BUSY
DYING

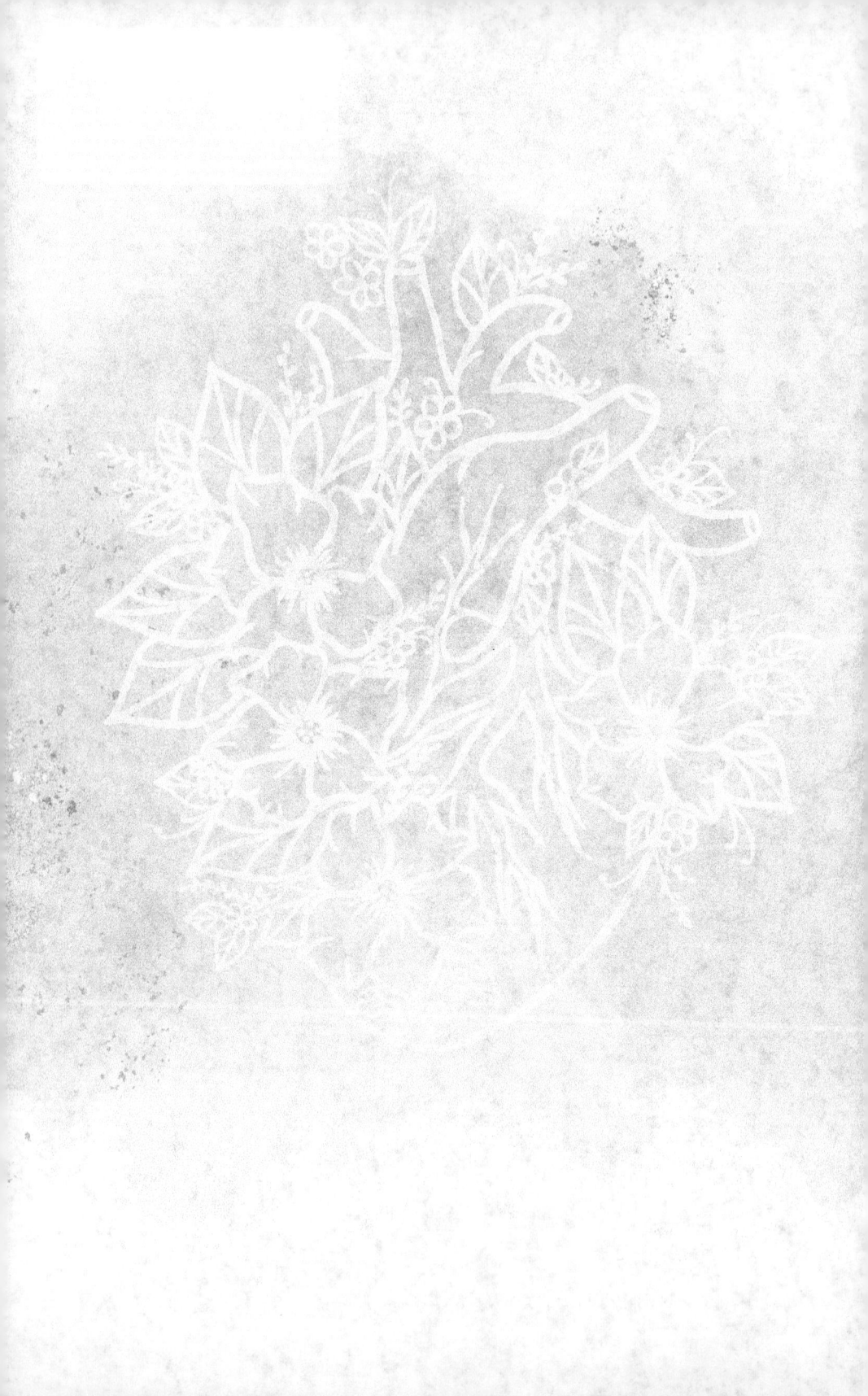

BUSY DYING

An Inspirational Memoir

KATHLEEN ROSE

Rose Garden
PUBLISHING

For information contact:
authorklr@gmail.com

Published by:
Rose Garden Publishing

Copy Editor: Kim Autrey • neveralonepublishing.com
Content Editor: Debbie Ihler Rasmussen • AuthorDebbieIhlerRasmussen.com

Cover design by Trivuj • 99designs.com

Interior book design by
Francine Platt, Eden Graphics, Inc. • edengraphics.net

Paperback ISBN 979-8-89454-003-0
eBook ISBN 979-8-89454-004-7

Library of Congress Number: Pending

Manufactured in the United States of America

First Edition

Dedicated to
Author Mary Flint

CHAPTER 1

Dying

IN STUNNED SILENCE, I stared out the window from my hospital bed. The sun cast bright rays on a large leafy tree growing just outside the window. Its branches housed a nest of newly hatched hungry robins, and their mother dangled a juicy worm from her beak.

Red tulips and yellow daffodils formed a perfect edging for the lush green grass before it met with the sidewalk. A collie dashed to catch a red ball being tossed by a young, blonde-haired man wearing a blue polo shirt. With delight, the dog would run, retrieve the toy, and return to its master.

Several joggers passed the window, and children eating popsicles played on the grass. Two yellow butterflies lingered on a lavender clematis bloom that was almost touching the glass. The world outside seemed full of the promise of spring and the bounty of new life.

Funny how one thin wall could separate two vastly different worlds.

On this side, my world of sixty-eight years would soon be ending. The cardiologist's words explaining the failed heart procedure were still fresh in my mind.

"Kathleen, we were unable to apply any stents. Many of the blood vessels are already calcified, preventing us from cleaning them out. Your heart valve is significantly damaged and is unable to pump blood completely into the left side. It's backflushing and is extremely enlarged and congested. There is not enough room in your chest for your lungs to completely expand, causing your shortness of breath. Your heartbeat is very irregular and weak, and your blood pressure is extremely high, causing more stress and damage to the valve, overworking your heart. Your kidneys…blah blah blah."

Doctor Barton kept talking, but I wasn't really listening anymore.

The list of health disappointments went on and on, diabetes, losing kidney function, and other complications.

Previously, the cardiologist, Dr. Flores, had talked to me in great detail about the dangerous risks of this procedure. Believing the benefits outweighed the risk, I had put all my faith in it. The procedure required I remain awake, and while in the operating room, I heard the surgeon and his assistant discussing that continuing was no longer an option. My target vessels were already too clogged and calcified. Since my heart valve was also damaged, it was time to stop the procedure.

The diagnosis was congestive heart failure confirming all anticipated fears about my health. To hear how futile the procedure had been pushed my mind into a dark and deep abyss.

Dr. Barton stood next to my bed and advised, "We'll try a combination of drugs to slow your heartbeat, allowing more time to empty the blood from one chamber to another. We'll test some specific drugs to see if they can help, but it will take time to adjust to correct dosages."

He sighed and briefly looked away. "We're going to observe you here in recovery for six more hours or so, then release you." He turned back to face me; his blank expression had not changed. "There's really not much more that Dr. Reed and I can do. We've already scheduled your follow-up next week with Dr. Allen. We used the artery in your right upper leg to access your heart. Nurse Kelly will be in shortly to talk with you about how to care for the incision. Follow her instructions carefully. If you begin to bleed at home, lay down flat on the floor and have someone apply pressure to the artery, and have them call for an ambulance immediately. Although honestly, they probably won't make it in time, as you can bleed out in minutes. So, it's very important that you do nothing to cause that. We're adding nitroglycerin to your prescriptions; Nurse Kelly has already called it in and make sure you carry it with you always."

There was an uncomfortable silence, then he asked, "Do you have any questions before I go?"

His bedside manner needs serious work.

My entire body was shaking, but I forced myself to speak. "Yes, I do. Is this permanent, or can I do something to help improve my heart?"

"Kathleen, the damage is…well, it is what it is. The deterioration, especially to your heart valve, is irreversible. Our goal with the medications is to minimize the rate of further problems, however, we will just have to try and see what happens. Dr. Allen is a close friend of mine, and his office is in the next building. I have worked with him for many years, and I've already spoken to him about your case. He's a fine cardiologist."

Dr. Barton rapped the door with his knuckles, opened it, and glanced back at me. "Remember to follow Nurse Kelly's instructions."

Then he was gone.

I watched the door until it closed.

My husband had been holding my hand and gave it a familiar squeeze. I turned my attention to him. My troubled eyes rested on his tired face. This sweet man had stood by me for twenty-five years.

He leaned over and gently kissed my forehead.

"We'll get through this. We always do."

CHAPTER 2

The Cottage

IT'S SUCH A BEAUTIFUL JUNE DAY. Our garden is blooming with stunning flowers, and the rose bushes are especially wonderful. We have many species; Lincoln red, peppermint, lavender blue, and three different types of yellow. My favorite is a hybrid, where each petal has a red interior and a yellow exterior. From a distance the roses look yellow with a red trim.

My dear husband, Gary, planted it June 19, five years ago on my birthday. They have a delicious intoxicating fragrance, and the bush gently frames the doorway of my little writer's cottage.

Three years ago, I brought back some starts from my childhood home in southeastern New Mexico, and planted lovely purple, yellow, and white irises. They line the right side of the little retreat. When I was five years old, I helped my mother plant the originals. Every year she would separate the bulbs and plant them a few feet apart on our acre of land, then the next year they would multiply, forming a beautiful edge around our property. One of my favorite activities was to cut a fresh bouquet, put them in mother's favorite vase, and place it on our kitchen table.

My small backyard getaway is affectionately named Rose after my last name, but also for the beautiful roses that decorate it. When I became ill, my husband built it for me. He put all his love into creating it, so I would have a refuge from the storm.

I am in it now, writing about my experiences. Fifteen months have passed, and I'm happy to tell you that I no longer have an expiration date like a carton of milk. Last week, I had my echocardiogram and the follow-up with my cardiologist, Dr. Allen. He happily told me that all was good, and that my heart was working perfectly. He said to keep doing everything I had been doing, and to keep taking my meds.

He smiled at me. "Don't change a thing. If anything seems different at all, come see me. Otherwise, I'll see you in a year." He added with another smile, "And I *will* see you in another year."

Now I'd like to tell you my story about healing my broken heart.

Actually, my heart was broken physically, but it was also broken emotionally and had been for many years. When I thought I was going to die, with very little time left, I began realizing how unprepared I was to go.

One morning, I woke up with a terrible thought, *When I die, the sweet sisters from my church will come to help my husband, and my house is a mess! I need to get busy.*

That's when I made my plan, and I was committed to accomplishing it. First, I must fight to live as long as I could, and second, I needed to use that time as wisely as I could, so I would be ready when my time came.

I became *busy dying.*

I didn't want a new life, I just wanted to keep the one I had. But when I became *busy dying* I not only got to keep my life, but now I have a better life.

This is my story.

CHAPTER 3

Fuel

AFTER MY FAILED HEART PROCEDURE, I returned home. For the next few days, I sat quietly staring at the TV from my comfy recliner. The screen became a blur as I faded into a world of my own thoughts, of my life's experiences. I had pushed the memories deep inside in an attempt to suppress them all. I had tried to hide them somewhere less reachable.

Now they found their way to the front of my mind's vision. Memories of pure sadness surfaced first. Then my waking reality set in causing shortness of breath, pains in my body, and extreme fatigue. I was brought back to my present dying world.

Gary handed me a glass of water and a small container filled with nine prescription pills. "Are you okay, sweetheart? I'm just coming to check on you, and I brought your morning meds." He touched my hand. "I made breakfast for us."

I was so tired, but I smiled. "Thank you, Gary."

I wanted to get up and do something, but what? My body and my mind were so exhausted. I just wanted to sleep, really rest, and not dream. Dreams can be full of bad things, and I didn't *need bad things* right now.

Gary cheerfully placed my breakfast on a folding stand. "Here you go. I hope you like it."

It did look delicious. Bacon, eggs, buttered pancakes with maple syrup, and a glass of milk. He took my hand and blessed the food. We enjoyed our breakfast together, and he removed the trays.

"I'll be outside mowing the lawn but let me know if you need anything."

Depressed and bored, I turned on the TV.

I spoke into the remote, "Congestive heart failure on YouTube."

A plethora of heart images filled the screen. I clicked on the first one, and a vivid diagram of two types of heart failure appeared: systolic and diastolic. Systolic or cardiac output is where the left ventricle cannot squeeze the blood out hard enough, causing some blood to remain in the left ventricle. It builds up pressure and forces fluids from your body into your lung tissues making it difficult to breathe. Diastolic is when the heart is squeezing hard enough, but not getting sufficient blood.

Lucky me, had *both* conditions, but primarily systolic heart failure.

I was irritated. *Show me something I don't already know.*

I clicked the next one and then the next. Each one was more depressing.

Where are the instructions. The ones that tell you how to get better.

I tried again. *Hmmmm, "Remedies for congestive heart failure."*

Many options popped up. I chose several more. I needed to be a medical grad student to understand them, but they all indicated that congestive heart failure was caused by multiple systems failing. Everything intertwined. Multiple causes for high blood pressure, diabetes, deteriorating blood vessels, also affected everything else. I was truly overwhelmed. I felt like I was drowning in a giant swimming pool.

The biggest culprit was obesity. I had been trying to lose weight for years. I could lose up to twenty-five pounds, but over time, I always gained it back. My current weight was two hundred and twenty pounds.

Dr. Allen was quick to tell me that my weight was my worst problem. I assumed that part of my treatment would include help from a dietitian, but recently, my insurance had changed to Medicare so that option was no longer covered. Losing weight seemed impossible.

The delicious breakfast that my husband had just made was killing us both. He was also a diabetic, only he was type 1 and I was type 2.

My heart condition had been originally discovered by Dr. Chakrabarti, my pulmonologist. I was referred to him because I was having difficulty breathing. I had suffered from COVID several times, and my primary doctor believed that was the issue. However, my pulmonary specialist identified my problem immediately and referred me to a cardiologist that he knew well.

The waiting time for a new patient appointment with the cardiologist was nearly six months. Dr. Chakrabarti said I would not live that long. He personally contacted Dr. Simms and told him if he did not see me next week, he would immediately hospitalize me until he could. Fortunately, I did see Dr. Simms right away, and he scheduled my heart procedure for the following week.

I rolled my eyes and blurted into the remote, "Healthy ways to lose weight on YouTube."

All sorts of choices popped up. Some promised instant results, others seemed even more ridiculous. But then, I watched one about cleaning out your blood vessels. It was not actually about losing weight. In theory, it was possible to significantly reverse heart damage. When you eat foods that help your body to fully function properly, you can beat diabetes, high blood pressure, obesity, and many other things without having to measure food and count calories. Over time the weight will adjust itself.

This was my *aha* moment. I needed to find out more about how my body really functioned and how to fuel every part of it. This was not about starving to lose weight. This was about fuel!

CHAPTER 4

Disappointment

I SAT STRAIGHT UP IN BED reeling from a recurring nightmare. It was the one where everything was desolate and burned up. Charred images of nutcrackers haunted me. The once brightly painted characters were now nothing more than charcoal silhouettes. I touched them, and they crumbled into piles of ashes. Anything I touched turned into dust. The filthy air burned my eyes, and they watered, impairing my vision.

A terrible acrid smell typical of an electrical fire was so pungent I could taste burnt plastic and metal. My throat burned, and I struggled to breathe. I choked and covered my face with a scarf to keep the ashes out of my eyes. The intense heat caused many household items to melt, looking as if they were in a surrealistic Salvador Dali painting.

My refrigerator door melted and then cooled when the water hoses flooded the house dousing the fire. Terrifying images of liquified metal immediately resolidified, becoming frozen in time. The melted cuckoo clock dripped down the wall before it met its final stage. My iron, once a solid metal piece that had served me for years, now lay in an unrecognizable, distorted form. I stumbled over it searching for a passageway through this cataclysm.

Burning beams that once supported the floor cracked and moaned under my feet. I tried to get out quickly, but they gave way, and I plummeted to the basement.

I crashed in a heap on burnt debris, and mangled pipes pierced me like medieval spears. Overwhelming pain consumed my broken body; despair and blackness overpowered me.

I knew this dream well.

It was only a slight piece of the actuality of the fire I had already experienced. This reality was set in stone, and there was nothing I could ever do to change it. In my waking hours I could control not dwelling on it, but while sleeping, my mind had a different agenda.

I squeezed my eyes shut and then quickly opened them. I could hear Gary in the kitchen making breakfast. Years of serving in the military had made him an early riser. I always knew when he was worried about me because he made breakfast. He is twelve years my senior and has the unique value system that a good husband never discusses unchangeable problems. Things in the past are out of our reach, and to prevent them from causing further damage, they should remain there. He is a rather quiet man, not too wordy. However, when he is with family or friends, he is caring, fun-loving, and witty.

I was relieved to be awake and no longer dreaming.

Unfortunately, I was back to reality, with my congestive heart failure. I quickly dressed as I had several upcoming medical appointments, and two of them were today. First, I had a forty-five-minute physical rehabilitation appointment at eight o'clock. It would take forty minutes to drive there. I had an assessment evaluation in the same hospital complex to determine my physical and mental health needs and learn about programs available to me. I was hopeful that someone could help me with my weight issues.

The directions we had been given were not sufficient, however, we optimistically made it to my first appointment, but then we had difficulty locating the rehab center. When we finally went inside, I observed patients using some of the simple workout equipment, completely unassisted. A few treadmills, two arm cycles, a rowing machine, and a stairstepping device.

I scoffed. *Well, this is curious.*

Gary took a seat in the waiting room, and I checked in for my appointment at the desk, then followed a bubbly girl to a room where she left me alone.

It wasn't long before a young man greeted me with a clipboard. "Hello, my name is James. I will be your evaluator today." He handed me some forms. "Fill these out and give them to the girl at the desk. She will let me know when you're finished, and I'll be back to set up your physical routine."

He smiled and left me with my assignment.

The forms were primarily a questionnaire with multiple-choice questions. Many were about diets and habits, but the problem was that none of these questions or their answers applied to me. I had already adjusted my diet, and so there was nothing here that fit what I was doing. For example, it asked me what I ate for dessert at each meal and gave me a list ranging from cakes, pies, ice cream, and cheesecake, to different kinds of cookies.

I sighed. *I no longer even eat dessert.*

Next was snacks. The list ranged from crackers, cheese, candy bars, and so on. One question asked, "Of the following items, how many times do you eat them in a week?" None of these questions applied to me as I no longer ate any of them. I stood and motioned to James, who was in the hall. I wanted to know how I should answer these questions as there was no space given for me to fill in an accurate response.

"Do you need help with something?"

"Yes." I pointed to the clipboard. "None of the multiple-choice answers apply to me, and I don't see a place to write a correct one. What would you recommend?"

"Let me see. I think you can just circle the choice that is nearest to your answer. Cheese and crackers don't have a lot of sugar. Candy bars do. If you eat snacks with a lot of sugar, you can circle candy bars. That would be close enough." He smiled and nodded curtly.

"The snacks that I eat are only fruits and vegetables. There are no similar choices."

He reached for the clipboard, and I handed it to him. "Are you sure? Sometimes our clients don't realize how many different snacks they're eating." He looked doubtful. "Perhaps you haven't really been keeping track. We have food diary forms to help you with that. I can give you one before you leave."

A sinking feeling came over me. I felt like he didn't think I was being honest.

I explained, "I have recently changed my diet, and I want this evaluation to be accurate, so I can get the help I need. I would like to schedule an appointment with a dietitian today."

He paused, gave me a forced smile, and explained, "We no longer have a dietitian on staff at this location, but it is still necessary for you to fill out the paperwork to qualify for rehab. It does not need to be exact as no one really ever reads them so just circle anything to fill it in. It is important for you as a client to realize that weight loss depends on what you eat. If you're not honest with yourself, you will not be successful in losing the extra weight you are carrying."

He handed the clipboard back to me.

I don't remember the last thing James said. I felt as if someone had slapped me and was talking down to me as if I had no idea I needed to lose weight. My mouth was dry, and I just wanted to disappear.

I looked down at the clipboard. The responses and choices for the mental health portion were even more confusing. I was uncomfortable with circling any of their predetermined answers. I returned the forms to the desk. Another young man gave me an explanation of the equipment. After a ten-minute workout, the receptionist made six 8:00 a.m. twenty-minute, weekly appointments. After that, I could schedule more. My insurance would allow fifty-six appointments that would cost two hundred and fifty dollars each. I was expected to sign in and work out independently.

I returned to the lobby where Gary was waiting for me. He stood. "Well, how did it go?"

I scowled. "I don't think this is going to work."

He took my arm, opened the door, and guided me out. "Really, why is that?"

"Well, first of all, I don't see much benefit in getting up at seven o'clock in the morning, driving forty minutes out here for a twenty-minute workout that I do totally on my own, and then driving forty minutes back home."

"You're kidding, that's the rehab program? That's it?"

"Pretty much, and *secondly,* there is absolutely no nutritional help. They not only confirmed that my insurance does not pay for a nutritionist, but they don't even have one. I asked them if I could weigh on their scale, and they don't have that either. What health place doesn't have a scale? Unbelievable!"

"Did you see a doctor? Surely, he or she told you something." He opened the car door for me, and I climbed in. He got in his door and started the engine.

I continued, "I didn't see a doctor. I saw a twenty-something assistant for about fifteen minutes. Also, I don't have another appointment today. I didn't feel comfortable filling out the mental health evaluation form. It was multiple choices with predetermined answers. I don't like having their answers become a permanent part of my medical records. By not filling out the form, I'm no longer eligible for their *delightful* program."

Gary raised his eyebrows; he seemed a little amused at my sarcasm. "I'm sorry it didn't work out for you. This whole thing sounds stressful, and the last thing you need in your life right now is more stress. I can help you work out an exercise program, and we can do things together like taking walks. You need a break from all of this and to get out of the house." He gave me one of his encouraging smiles, reached over, patted my leg, and continued.

"I have an idea. How about I take you out for an early lunch. We can go to that Chinese buffet you like."

I frowned. "No. How about we go to Costco instead. I need to buy some canned tuna, broccoli, and blueberries."

He winked at me. "Oh yum, I can't wait. That sounds like a great lunch."

"No silly." I laughed and poked his arm. "We can get something at the food court. I just can't eat sugar, fat, or salt."

"Well, that doesn't leave much." He scrunched his face. "What can you eat?"

"Things that are lean, green, and purple."

"That sounds like you're a goat."

"That's not all. I just need to add more of these things. It has to do with nitric oxide."

"Nightside what?" He was teasing me now.

"Nothing. It's just something I learned on YouTube. I'll explain it later."

Obviously pleased with himself he said, "At least I got a smile out of you. We're here. Let's go get some tasty green and purple stuff!"

He was right. I did need to take a break and get out of the house. While shopping, I was getting very tired and clinging to the grocery cart as if it was a walker. We stopped at the pharmacy and picked up two new prescriptions for me, then at the food court, Gary got a slice of pizza and a Pepsi. I got a tossed green salad with tomatoes and chicken breast slices with a low-calorie dressing.

"Do you want a diet cola?" he offered.

"No thanks, just water please." It was so tempting. That was my favorite drink. I'm sure my medical records listed diet cola for my blood type. I used to drink it constantly, but now I needed to break my addiction, and artificial sweeteners were off my list. My liquid intake had been reduced as well because I had to weigh myself twice a day to monitor my heart congestion. If I were to drink too much, it could show my congestion was getting really bad.

If I suddenly gained any weight in a twenty-four-hour period, I needed to see my doctor or go to the emergency room immediately.

We enjoyed our lunch and went home. Gary helped me into the house and sat down with me on the reclining sofa in our family room. I was terribly exhausted. My head ached, I felt dizzy, and I started coughing. This was a symptom that my lungs were failing to fully expand. After a few minutes, I had some discomfort in my chest.

Gary looked concerned. "Do you need to go to the emergency room, Kathleen."

I took a deep breath. "Let's wait a few minutes and see if the pain gets any worse." I tried to give him a smile to reassure him I was just fine, but it didn't work.

"Let's take your blood pressure to make sure something bad isn't happening." He wrapped the cuff around my left arm. The reading was very high. He waited a few minutes and took it again. The pain in my chest had diminished leaving just a tight achy feeling. This time the reading was much lower.

He tenderly stroked my hair. "Are you okay now? Is it better?"

"Yes, I think I'll be alright now. I'm just tired."

I kept my nitroglycerin in my purse, and Gary put it beside me. He handed me the TV remote. "I'm leaving your phone here, and I'll keep mine in my pocket. Call me if you need anything."

I moved my phone next to my purse. "Okay, where are you going?"

"I'll just be cleaning the garage. Try to get some rest." Gary kissed my forehead and went outside.

I spoke into the remote, "YouTube." I searched through options when my phone rang.

"Hi, Mom, how did your appointments go? Did you get to see a dietitian like you wanted?"

"No, Maisie, I didn't. I was misinformed that they had one."

"Well, that's a bummer. You sound upset, are you okay?"

"I don't know, I guess I am."

"I know you were hopeful about getting some help with your weight. How did the rest of the appointments go?"

"Nothing to write home about. The rehab center was a big disappointment. It was just an insurance money making mill. Oh well, it's probably for the better. It was a long drive out there anyway. How was your day?"

"Grant took the girls to help at the animal rescue farm in Heber. Chloe really likes to help with the chickens and rabbits. Sometimes they let Sophie ride a horse, so they were excited to go with their dad for the day."

"What are you doing?"

"I stayed home to catch up on things. I do have some good news to share with you. I stopped at Organ Donor's Memorial Park today, and they added new names to the wall. Jared's name is on it now."

"Oh… That's so nice. I wondered when they would add more. How does it look?"

"Really nice, Mom. They did a good job, and it's easy to find. I'll take you up there soon because I think you would enjoy it. They added a fountain, some new benches, and the park is pretty with all the flowers in bloom. We could take a lunch and stay awhile."

"I'd like that, Maisie. When I feel a little better, we should go."

"Mom, you sound really tired, so I'll let you get some rest. Give my love to Gary."

"I will. Love you, honey, bye bye."

"Love you too, Mom, bye."

CHAPTER 5

Consolation

MY MIND began to fill with memories of Maisie, now forty-seven, and Jared, who would have been forty-three. The last time I saw him, he was fourteen. They were a fun-loving, close pair. Blue-eyed Maisie with her long blonde hair, and brown marble-eyed Jared, with his dark umber hair, made quite a lovely sight. They were best friends and always took care of each other. Despite being products of divorced parents, they found ways to be happy. Their dad, my ex-husband, was a financial alcoholic who was addicted to "get rich quick schemes" as well as gambling in the stock market. He lost thousands of dollars and sold our house out from under us to pay his debts. Abuse and infidelity were also a part of his résumé, and court obligations such as medical expenses, insurance, and child support, were always in arrearage. He rarely saw Maisie and Jared.

My mind began locating memories that had brought

much joy to my life. A quiet calm accompanied these thoughts as I let myself rest in them. I began to peacefully drift off to sleep, but in dreaming, my subconscious would alter my blissful view.

It was a breezy fall Saturday as colorful leaves fluttered their way to the ground. Twelve-year-old Jared and his friend, Randy, had walked to our local grocery store. Maisie was off with some classmates volunteering at the local animal shelter. I was busy giving my Saturday piano and violin lessons.

Caitlin, my first student, looked so festive in her shiny new pink satin dress her mother made for her sixth birthday. Her curly red hair accentuated her massive pink bow.

When Caitlin arrived, she had accidentally let Rhett, the neighbor's terrier, in our house. She mistakenly thought Rhett was our dog anxiously waiting on the porch. The dog spooked Prissy, Maisie's black cat who lunged off the couch and crash landed on Rhett.

Barking furiously, Rhett chased Prissy, who took refuge by jumping up onto my grand piano. The startled feline hit so forcefully that the lid fell, locking her inside. Not to miss the excitement, Tank, our little pug, joined in the fun play by attacking Rhett.

Tank bumped Caitlin, knocking her piano book out of her hand. Bewildered, she bent down to retrieve it, but tripped over Rhett, and fell into the floor lamp, crashing it into pieces. Her pretty pink bow fell off, landing at

Tank's feet, who immediately tore it to shreds.

My neighbor, Jan, called through the screen door, "Has anybody seen Rhett?"

I snatched the destroyed bow from Tank and scooped Rhett up while Prissy screamed from inside the piano.

"Come on in, Jan, and join the fun." I smiled and handed Rhett to her.

"Oh no! Did you do all of this, Rhett?" Jan gasped and pushed him away, so he was out of her face's licking range.

"Oh, trust me, he had help." I lifted the piano lid releasing an angry cat who darted out of the room.

Jan's eyes widened. "Thanks, Kathleen, I have to run."

I waved to Jan. Caitlin was gathering broken pieces of the lamp.

"I'm sorry, I didn't mean to break it."

"Oh, don't worry, Rhett and Tank are the ones who did it." I smiled and helped her clean up. "I'm sorry about your pink bow. I'll help your mom get you another one."

Caitlin shrugged. "That's ok, I don't mind. Tank really likes it."

We both turned to the sofa where the delighted dog guarded a mass of pink ribbon between his paws.

Caitlin giggled and I laughed.

"Well, we had better start your piano lesson now. I'm excited to hear how you're doing with *Rhinos in the Mud.*"

Caitlin proudly played it for me, and we finished her lesson. Three more students came that day.

During the last lesson, Jared and Randy burst through the front door and abruptly headed downstairs where Jared's room was.

I knew immediately that something was wrong.

I called down the stairs, "Jared, I made some of your favorite chocolate chip cookies." I waited for an answer but heard nothing. I added a little louder, "I have ice cream, too, if you and Randy would like to come up and have some."

I waited another five minutes, but still no answer.

This time I yelled, "Hey, Jared, is everything alright down there? The ice cream is going to melt."

Randy answered, "We're fine, thanks. We'll be up in a minute."

Now I knew something was wrong. I made two plates of the treats and placed them on the table next to two glasses of milk. When Randy and Jared came in the kitchen, I noticed Jared's swollen red eyes. He had been crying. Trying not to pry or embarrass him, I smiled and set the entire container of cookies in front of them.

"Have all you want. There's plenty more. You doing okay, Jare?"

"Yeah, Mom, sure. I'm fine." He gave his face a quick wipe with his sleeve.

Randy gave Jared a little poke with his elbow. "No, you're not. Tell her what Jerk Face did to you in the store."

I was puzzled. "Jerk Face? Who are you talking about? What happened?"

"That's what Randy calls Dad. It's alright, Mom. I don't really care about what happened. Just forget it."

Randy pressed harder. "No. How can you forget it? He treated you like trash. My parents are divorced, too. I don't see my dad very much either, but when I do, he's always glad to see me and treats me nice."

Pain was written all over Jared's face.

His father had a new girlfriend. I knew that he still lived in the area, but we hadn't heard from him in several months. I thought he was just dodging child support.

I pulled a chair over and sat down by Jared. "Would you like to tell me about it, son?"

Jared took a deep breath, then rolled his eyes.

"We were walking down an aisle in Smith's grocery store, and I saw Dad. I thought he would be glad to see me, so I went over to say hi. He looked surprised and pulled me around the corner to another aisle. He said he couldn't talk to me and that I needed to leave *now*. I asked him why. He said he was there with Meredith. He didn't want her to see me because she didn't know about me. He pushed me away, and then waved at me to leave. I didn't want to go, so he shoved five dollars in my hand and told me to get away. He went and hid somewhere in the store, so Randy and I left."

I put my arms around him, and we both began to cry.

Randy leaned over and hugged his friend.

CHAPTER 6

Buying Time

GARY WALKED INTO THE ROOM and pulled me out of my thoughts. Tears streamed down my face, and I wiped them away as I got up to take my second set of pills.

He had bought me a new digital scale, and I weighed myself.

This can't be right. It's probably not adjusted correctly. I've lost sixteen pounds in the last three weeks. That's crazy! Maybe I have. Oh well, they will weigh me when I see the Dr. Allen tomorrow.

Three weeks ago, I constructed a new diet for myself based on my last blood test that had indicated several serious deficiencies. These included a severe lack of vitamins D and B12, magnesium, and potassium. My blood sugar was also extremely high. I began eating bananas with Ceylon cinnamon as well as fresh berries, particularly strawberries and blueberries. More fruits, and vegetables such as leafy greens like kale and broccoli to raise my nitric oxide level, necessary for strengthening the lining of my blood vessels. I included fish, nuts, and lean proteins in my diet. I ate grains and other carbs sparingly in addition to cutting out all added salt, sugar, and grease. My biggest challenge was giving up diet soda.

For years I thought I was on a healthier path by drinking diet beverages instead of their sugared counterparts. I found out through my research that it was far worse to drink diet beverages because they cause multiple health problems such as insulin resistance and rob your bones of phosphorus and calcium. I began exercising and taking walks regularly. Unbelievably after four days of following my new diet, my blood sugar levels were at perfect readings. I kept researching congestive heart failure, and I put into practice everything I learned.

Gary asked me, "What time is your doctor's appointment?"

"It's at one thirty, but I need to be there by one. Sometimes it takes a while to check in."

"Is this with Dr. Flynn at the clinic?"

"No, that was last week. Today, it's Dr. Allen. His office is in the building next to the Riverton hospital."

"Oh, that's right. You have so many appointments I have a hard time keeping them all straight. So, what exactly is this one for?"

"Mainly to see if my medications are working. He might adjust my dosages. Oh, I meant to ask you, is my scale calibrated?"

"It sure is. I did that right after I put the new batteries in."

"I just wondered because it says I have lost sixteen pounds in the last three weeks. I don't think that sounds right."

"Well, that's a good thing, isn't it?"

I agreed, but it still seemed odd.

Despite the lunch hour traffic, we arrived early and conveniently found a handicapped parking space. After signing in, I had a relatively short wait before the nurse called my name.

"How are you today?" She held the door open for me.

"I'm fine." I followed her to the scale, took my shoes off, and stepped on.

She pushed a button to reset it. "Let's see. …198.5 lb. Looks like you've lost some weight."

I was surprised. "Are you sure that's right? That means I've lost twenty-two pounds."

"Yes, that's right." She smiled. "Have a seat. I'll come back and get you when Dr. Allen is ready."

It wasn't long before the doctor came in. "Hello. What do we have here?" He looked at my chart then twisted his mouth. "What's this? You've lost twenty-two pounds. Are you following one of those terrible fad diets?"

Here it comes.

I sat up straight. "No, I'm not."

"Well, that's good. Those kinds of diets can kill a person. What are you doing?"

"I'm not really doing a particular diet. I mainly changed my eating habits. I've stopped eating sugar, fats, and no added salt. I'm eating lots of fresh fruits, and vegetables, fish, and a little lean chicken. I also started an exercise routine."

"Sounds like a great plan, seems to be working. Let's check your heart." He placed his stethoscope on my chest. "It sounds the same. I can still hear the congestion and the four murmurs, and your heartbeat is still uneven and weak."

He looked at my chart again, then asked, "Have you been having any pains?"

"I still have a few, but not like I did before I had my procedure."

"That's good. I'll have the nurse take your vitals before you leave, so we can add the results to your record. Keep up with your new diet. Schedule at the desk to see me in another month."

The ride home was quiet. Gary and I didn't quite know what to think about the results of the appointment. I was happy that I had lost weight, but after all my efforts, everything with my heart was still the same. At least the doctor thought I was well enough that I didn't have to come back for a month.

My appointments had gone from weekly to bi-weekly, and now an entire month. That in itself was an improvement.

CHAPTER 7

Temptation

STAYING TRUE TO MY DIET was extremely difficult. I never realized just how much unhealthy food there was around me. It was everywhere. Hamburger or fried chicken food chains on every corner, ice cream, donut shops, pizza, aisles in the grocery stores, food courts, concession stands, amusement parks, movie theatres, school and community fund raisers, family get-togethers, and church activities— all offering food I should not eat. So much of our culture is based on feeding people. Food is given as gifts, signs of friendship or hospitality, or expressions of sympathy. Sometimes refusing to accept such offers offends the giver and can even be viewed as an insult.

The temptation is strong to eat those yummy looking things.

I developed a strange self-protective mechanism. Whenever I saw someone eating unhealthy food, I would see a bite going down the person's throat into their digestive system as if watching a kind of internal medical video. I imagined the food breaking down and going to all parts of the body and then magnified. I could see a rise in blood pressure as the heart muscle began beating faster as it struggled to pump more oxygen-rich blood throughout their body. The pressure inside the arteries and veins began to tear away the lining in prelude of a heart attack. I saw the depletion of their insulin, nitric oxide, and vital vitamins, causing further damage to their vessels, lungs, liver, and kidneys.

These imaginary videos served as a great deterrent for me.

To further the problem of resisting, many people often insisted that I eat lovely, delectable foods. For example, I went to an event at my local church. The entire neighborhood had been invited, and the cookie experts were out in full force. They provided two large refreshment tables filled with a plethora of huge cookies that looked more like candy bars. They also offered little cartons of chocolate milk. The display could qualify for a PBS cookie bakeoff!

Near the end of that evening, although the event had been a success, boxes of uneaten cookies were left over. As Gary and I were leaving, we were intercepted by two of our church ladies, each holding two boxes of cookies.

Maeve offered her two dozen. "Here, Kathleen, these are for you and your husband."

I had already declined her delicious treats earlier that evening.

"Oh, no thank you. You're very kind, but we can't eat them for health reasons." I lightly pushed away the cookies.

She plopped her boxes into my husband's hands. "I know you can't eat them, but Gary can."

"No, he can't." I promptly took the boxes from Gary and handed them back to her.

Maeve peered around the stack. "Well, then share them with your neighbors. It's a good way to fellowship." She handed the boxes back to Gary.

Trying not to show my irritation, I took the boxes from Gary and gave them back again.

Referring to her two teenage children, I said, "That would be a good opportunity for Richard and Chelsea."

Still pressing, Maeve said, "They're really busy with activities these days. I still think you should take them."

Gary took my hand. "I'm sorry, we really do have to go. See you ladies at church Sunday." He hurried me out the door.

When we got home, we sat down to watch our favorite TV show.

I turned to Gary. "What do you think that was all about?"

"What was what all about? Oh, you mean the cookies. That happens to you all the time. Haven't you figured it out yet?"

"No, not really. I just don't want cookies sitting around tempting us. It's hard enough as it is. And besides, I don't want to give them to our neighbors. To me, it's the same as giving someone cigarettes."

Gary turned to face me. "Honey, you really don't understand. You have lost a lot of weight, and it's beginning to show. You've received compliments lately. You're not exactly on Brenda and Maeve's 'I love you list.' They both have large weight problems. They probably would have liked for you to stay as you were. Besides, they get a lot of baking compliments, and their self-esteem depends on it. They probably took your *cookie* refusal as an insult."

"I know, but it's hard for me when they plan these things for church. They always pass around a sign-up sheet for specific items to bring. For the sundae party, we were asked to bring a certain brand of ice cream and toppings. If I don't sign up, they find me later, personally hand me the clip board, and point out the remaining items to choose from. It's not like they have any other options for someone like me. When I don't eat anything, I get teased about it. They don't understand how sick I am, and I don't want to explain it to them. I'm just tired of being pushed."

"I know, I see when they do that to you. I think we should just stay home from those functions."

He watched me for a few seconds, then said, "Okay, our show is on now. Are you ready?"

I smiled, I tried to hide my disappointment, but I already felt isolated from that group of ladies. They had been friends for over thirty years. It was impossible to put a dent in their little clique.

CHAPTER 8

Stuck in a Loop

OVER THE NEXT FEW WEEKS, I completely reorganized my life. I wanted to utilize every moment. I made a list of my top priorities and among those included special time with my husband and family members. I made sure that my list was reasonable and realistically doable. I didn't want to become overwhelmed and fail.

I started a new page with the heading "Downsizing."

Gary and I moved from Alaska a few years ago, but we still had boxes we hadn't opened. Some were even still out in the storage shed. We purchased new items, duplicating some things we already had, such as a new dining room table. The old set was still good, so we put it downstairs in the basement. Sometimes, we bought sale items for the simple reason they were on sale, and besides, they would make good gifts.

There are numerous reasons for accumulating things, but never enough reasons for getting rid of them. The pitfall is that it's easy to forget about the extras until you decide to sort through them. Then it's like rediscovering old friends, and the attachment is there all over again.

"Oh wow, look! I remember when we got these on the kids' first trip to Disneyland."

"I forgot I even had these. They would make good gifts."

"This was Mom's."

And it goes back on the shelf, even though there is no practical functional purpose—*today*. Sometimes you might not know what to do with it, and you don't want to throw it away because it is still good, so it goes to the storage room, or maybe the closet, just for now, probably better in the garage. Soon every spare living space is consumed. As a child, I learned to save things for economic reasons. When I was a single mother, every penny counted. I developed financially helpful practices that continued throughout my life, but now they had become counterproductive habits.

It's depressing to live in a messy house, but it's also difficult to clean a cluttered house, so, often people alienate themselves from friends and family to hide their living conditions. Self-esteem diminishes, discouragement sets in, and any interest in improving their surroundings is discarded.

As a busy working single mother, I had often fallen into this trap. My dishes were done, laundry was clean, and the living room picked up for piano lessons, but that was about it. I worked long hours at my job, taught piano lessons on Saturdays, and was exhausted at the end of every day. Between church, school, and family, life was always in the fast lane.

It was exhausting just thinking about it, so I opened the pantry door to get a dish scrubby so I could load the dishwasher.

Things had been shuffled all over the place.

How did the garbage bags get on top of the flour? And why is the dishwashing liquid with the bottles of vegetable oil?

It was time for a total reset, but I promptly made a common mistake.

Completely ignoring what I opened the door for in the first place, I spent the next two hours cleaning and organizing the pantry. I did have a sense of pride when I finished, but I turned around to face the same messy kitchen.

I rolled my eyes. I remembered I was about to load the dishwasher. I bent over to open it and saw two dishtowels on the floor.

I'll just stick these in the washer with the bathroom towels to get that load going.

I grabbed a couple more items and tossed them into the washer.

Gary often helped me with laundry, and I discovered a pile of clean clothes folded neatly on top of the dryer.

I took the clothes downstairs to put them away before they got knocked to the floor.

On the way to our bedroom, I passed through the family room. Our son had friends over last night and left piles of leftover snacks, soda cans, and empty plates. I tossed the clean load of laundry onto the couch, hurriedly picked up the trash, gathered up the leftovers, and headed back upstairs.

Back in the kitchen, I threw away the trash, put the soda cans into the recycle bin, and finished loading the dishwasher.

I heard the garage door open, and shortly, Gary walked in. He placed his packages on the counter, then his face twisted into one of his cute funny looks.

"Uh, honey, have you been standing in that same spot for the last three hours? That's exactly where you were when I left."

I laughed. "No, I got a little distracted, but the pantry is clean, so don't mess it up. Remember, just because you find an empty space, it doesn't mean you get to fill it up."

"Oh, okay." Gary laughed, too. "It's almost five, did you remember the missionaries are coming for dinner?"

My startled face was a dead giveaway.

"You forgot," he chided. "They're coming at five-thirty. I'll go pick up some pizzas." He smiled, threw me a kiss, and disappeared into the garage.

CHAPTER 9

Seeds

I AM NOW IN ONE OF MY FAVORITE PLACES—my secret garden. The entryway is a small, enclosed arbor surrounded by lavender wisteria. It grows upward on a white lattice fence and extends to the roof and produces a deliciously fragrant smell. The moose on the wrought iron door was made in Clam Gulch, Alaska. Gary and I brought it here as a tribute to all the moose on our two-acre property in Bear Valley.

Once you enter and turn right, there is another arbor. The eight-foot edifice will soon produce tasty green and purple seedless grapes. The arbor connects to another garden that boasts thriving large blackberry bushes along a beige block fence that stands seven feet high. The opposite wall is a beautiful display of red and yellow rose bushes. A yellow bearing apple tree graces the center along with a lovely white garden chair and a writing table that beckon me to a welcome rest.

This is my special place of contemplation where I find peace and security. It is my refuge from the storm.

Last year, Gary built a small greenhouse in the backyard. It was mainly a seed starting nursery. This year, he built a larger one, so the seedlings had a place to grow into bigger plants. This would enable them to have a longer growing season and produce fruit sooner.

I learned about different varieties of seeds, and starting plants this way is more economical. Organic seeds, or conventional seeds are certified that no synthetics were used in growing them. However, sometimes the seeds they produce can be weaker because of exposure to diseases or pests. Plants that are stronger are typically treated with synthetic fertilizers.

I am often asked questions about gardening and seeds. These are some of the answers I have shared.

- GMO seeds or genetically modified organisms are bred in labs and not gardens to ensure a desired characteristic. These are not sold to the public.

- Non-GMO seeds are cultivated through pollination. They are either hybrid or open pollinated seeds.

- Hybrid seeds are offspring of two different plants with different characteristics. If you want to get the same plant again, you must purchase the same seeds. If you choose to save your own seeds and plant them, you will get the characteristics of only one parent plant.

- Heirloom seeds are produced from plants that have been the same for many generations to preserve stability

- Soil is also an important factor. Seeds cannot be planted deeper than twice their size because that is all the energy they have. Potting soil is the best because it has a small amount of fertilizer in it but not enough to burn the tiny plants. As the seedlings get bigger, they will need more fertilizer, or they will die. Sprinkling a little cinnamon over freshly planted seeds will keep mold from forming. Germinating seeds need moisture, and cinnamon has antibacterial agents.

We grow many vegetables including tomato, eggplant, pepper, kale, lettuce, squash, cucumber, and green bean plants. Adding Bing cherry trees, seedless grapes, strawberries, and blackberries provide more nutrients to our diet.

Having our own produce in a beautiful garden environment has enriched our lives, and we love to share our experiences with others. Some people have large gardens, and some have only a pot or two. Depending on the size, most vegetables can be grown in a pot, and flowerpots can enrich anyone's life.

CHAPTER 10

A Visitor in My Garden

WITHIN THE FIRST FOUR DAYS of changing my diet, my blood sugar levels changed to perfect readings. I was amazed at how fast this happened. Within two weeks, my feet were less painful and no longer swollen. After three weeks, my headaches had improved, and I could breathe easier.

I began concentrating on a better exercise program by adding cardio and endurance. Working in my garden provides clarity and rest to my mind and expected healthy food and even more exercise.

While working in my beautiful blooming roses, they filled my senses with their enjoyable fragrance, and the apple tree was full of lovely white blooms. I dug into a small patch of ground in preparation for planting a few of my seedlings. Spring is such a lovely time of year when everything comes alive again.

I thought I saw something on the ground under the apple tree. It looked like part of a thin rope or bungee cord with an intricately woven red and brown design. *I better pick it up, so it doesn't interfere with the lawn mower.* I changed my mind. *No, I better not because it just moved.*

Oh, it was a cute little garden snake! It had been a while since I had seen one. It scurried away into the grass behind the garden shed. That little snake reminded me of another one I saw many years ago.

When I was a single parent in my thirties, I purchased a small older home in an area known as Reed's Park. I resided there with my two children, Jared and Maisie.

Jared was eight and he loved snakes. He studied a lot and knew how to take care of them. He knew the difference between poisonous and non-poisonous types. Often, Jared and his friend, Chris, would go to the Jordan River Walkway to find a snake and bring it home for a visit. Jared knew that small garden snakes ate insects as part of their diet. After a few days, when the snake stopped eating, Jared and Chris would return it to the Jordan River area. Sometimes they would find another one and bring it home, too.

We had an apple tree in our front yard with blooms that attracted many bugs and insects. One day while I was mowing the lawn under that tree, I was surprised to come face-to-face with a garden snake dangling from a branch. When Jared came home from school and I told him about my experience, he informed me that the apple tree was the preferred lodging for his guest snakes.

The previous summer, Jared, Maisie, and I went to San Antonio, Texas, for a two-week vacation. It was June, and we were visiting my brother, John, and his wife, Anne, and would be there for my birthday. Their beautiful home, surrounded by a lush green lawn with lovely orange hibiscus flowers, resembled an oasis in the Texas desert. Jared immediately made friends with Carl, their family gardener.

A few days before my birthday, Jared began spending a lot of time with Carl in the backyard. I assumed he was helping him with some kind of gardening project. That afternoon, Jared ran into the house and breathlessly asked Anne if she had a shoebox. She accommodated him, and he disappeared in a flash. Through the window, we could see him talking with Carl, and it appeared they were planning something. Jared glanced up and saw us watching him. He and Carl took the shoebox and relocated where we could no longer see them.

My birthday was the next day, and Maisie, John, and Anne surprised me with a luncheon. The grass was freshly mowed, and they had decorated the patio with colorful streamers and balloons. The table was ladened with presents, picnic food, a beautifully decorated angel food cake, ice-cold lemonade, and soda. A few of John's and Anne's friends had been invited to celebrate with us.

After eating and sharing fun conversations, John invited me to open my presents. It was a family tradition to guess what the gift was before opening it.

"Okay." I held a large floral print bag from Anne, and I gently pressed the sides. "It feels soft, maybe a robe or a shawl." I opened the bag to find a light blue silky robe with pink roses embroidered on the sleeves.

I gave Anne a hug. "Thank you so much. I really need a new robe, and this one is very pretty."

Maisie excitedly handed me another floral bag. "Here, Mom. Open this one next." I could tell there were some small individual items inside.

"Let me guess." I carefully gave the bag a couple of good squeezes. "I think it might be lotion or perfume, maybe some makeup." I opened the bag. "Oh wow, Maisie. These are my favorite hair care products!"

Maisie grinned. "Aunt Annie helped me pick them out. They are her favorites, too."

"There are more gifts, but I think Jared is anxious for you to open his present next," said John. "I don't know what it is, but I've been assured by him that you're going to absolutely love it."

Jared handed me a shoebox wrapped in a modified paper bag. I could tell that my young son had put great effort into making the paper fit the box. It looked like he had used an entire dispenser of tape.

"I know you'll just love it, Mom, it's really neat. I can't wait for you to open it."

I could see the excitement in his face. It was obvious he had put a lot of time and effort into this gift, and he was so proud to give it to me.

I gave him a big smile and carefully pulled off a piece of tape. "I'm sure I will love it."

"No, wait, Mom. You didn't guess what it is."

"Oh, you're right. I was excited! Let me see. I think it's in a shoe box, but it's too light to be a pair of shoes. I can't press it in like a bag to feel something inside. Maybe I should shake it a little to get a hint."

"You can shake it," said Jared. "Just not too hard."

I lifted the box and lightly shook it. Something inside rolled around. I shook it again.

"Oh, this is interesting. It feels like something is moving around. It could be marbles."

Jared giggled. "No, Mom. There are no marbles. You'll never figure it out, so you might as well just open it."

"Well, don't give up on me yet. I'll shake it one more time, maybe a little harder."

"Okay, but you get only one more chance. This is your last guess."

I held it tightly and gave a really good shake. "It does feel like something could be moving inside. Is it a guinea pig?" I teased.

"No, Mom." He laughed. "That's your last guess. Now you have to open it."

I began removing the layers of tape. John took mercy on me and handed me a knife to cut the box open.

Jared jumped up. "Wait, Mom! Don't use a knife, I mean, it's better to just use your fingers."

I got through what seemed like yards of tape, I removed the bag, and I leaned down. I slowly opened the lid and peeked inside.

Suddenly something struck my face and latched onto the nosepiece of my glasses. I ripped them off to see a little garden snake clinging from the center.

Jared scrunched his face. "Oh, I guess he didn't like it when you shook the box. I put some rocks in it to make it more like his natural habitat. Do you like him, Mom? Is he a good present?"

I could see disappointment spreading across Jared's young face.

"Of course I like him," I blurted as adrenaline surged through my body. "I love him. He is a wonderful present and so cute." I still held the foot-long snake dangling from my glasses. "But I don't think he's happy in the box. Where did you find him?"

"Carl and I found him in the backyard in the apple tree. I think Snakie likes to eat the insects and bugs."

"Yep, that's where I'd want to be if I was a cute little garden snake. Why don't you put him back in the tree, and Uncle John can help you find a more suitable habitat for Snakie later, unless he moves to a better location on his own." I handed Jared my gift. "Don't forget to bring my glasses back."

Jared gave me a quick little hug and took the lively present. "I knew you would like it, Mom. I always know how to pick the right gifts for you because they always make you so happy."

"That's right, you know exactly what I like. Your presents always make me happy."

CHAPTER 11

Crime and Punishment

WHEN JARED WAS IN THE FOURTH GRADE, his teacher was Miss Peterson. She taught her group of nine-year-olds at Meadow Lark Elementary School located next to the Jordan River Walkway. After school on a beautiful day near the end of May when the year was about to end, Jared hurried home and ran in the house to find me.

"Mom!"

I called back, "I'm in the kitchen!" I walked into the living room where he was standing and asked him, "How was your day?"

Jared was laughing. "Mom, I need to tell you what happened at school today. It was too funny."

I motioned to the sofa. "Come sit down and tell me."

He took a deep breath and then started talking fast. "After we finished lunch and recess, we went back to class, and everybody was being noisy. Some students were talking about the substitute teacher that the other fourth-grade class has, and some of the kids were still standing up. Miss Peterson told us to sit down and work on our essays.

"She said don't forget they are due on Wednesday. We were still being rowdy, so she told us if we made noise or if we disobeyed the classroom rules, she would write our name on the board, and we wouldn't get to go on the field trip to get ice cream at the Dairy Barn.

"We all hurried and got to our desks, and we were really quiet. Then I worked on my English paper. We had to write about a family member or pet, so I started thinking about what to write. My desk is in the front right by the door, and I can see all the way to the outside."

I was chuckling inside watching his excited expressions.

Jared continued, "I saw something coming down the hall, and Mom," Jared's voice went up two octaves. "It was a snake! I thought it would go out the door, but all of a sudden, it came into our class. I couldn't tell if it was poisonous or not, so I just held really still. I thought about raising my hand, but I didn't want to bother Miss Peterson."

"Jared, it was a snake, I don't think she would get mad at you."

His eyes widened. "She said to be quiet, Mom."

I couldn't argue with that, so I just smiled. "You're right."

"The snake climbed up my desk and went inside! I didn't know what to do; I couldn't help it, so I yelled

Miss Peterson's name. She jumped up and slammed her book on her desk, and the whole class stared at me. But I could see the snake's head, so I held perfectly still. Miss Peterson looked at me kinda mad, and then she put my name on the board.

"The snake started moving, so I yelled, Miss Peterson! There's a snake in my desk! Some girls saw it, and they started screaming. Miss Peterson told me not to move and everyone to come to the front of the room, and she told Justin to go get Mr. Mason quick! Justin came back with Mr. Mason, and he was wearing gloves and had a bucket. He put the snake in it and borrowed my notebook to cover the top. We found out that Mr. Mason had brought the snake to show his class and it had escaped.

"Everyone sat down, and the whole class and Miss Peterson were looking at me. I felt bad seeing my name on the board because I wanted to go get ice cream. Miss Peterson said, we need to talk about yelling. If there's an emergency such as a snake in someone's desk, and you can prove it, then if you yell, I won't put your name on the board. Since Jared proved he had a snake in his desk, I'm erasing his name from the board right now."

Many years later, I still love to be in my garden. If it's a really good day, I might get a brief visit from a cute little guest in my apple tree.

CHAPTER 12

Death

The Destruction or Permanent End of Something

Wwhat had just happened? This can't be real! The voice screamed so loud, my head was pounding, and I felt like it was going to explode. The intolerable pain rushed all the way to my feet, and I began shaking uncontrollably. My lungs burned, and I could barely breathe.

"Please, someone help me!"

I was so dizzy I felt like I was falling off a cliff. My heart raced, my anxiety was suffocating me, and I struggled to catch my breath.

I screamed, "Make it stop. Please! Make it stop. Can't anyone help me?"

No one in the hospital waiting room even looked at me. I was screaming, but no sound was coming out of my mouth. I couldn't see clearly, and the dizziness was worse. I was going to pass out. I tried to stand to get to the nurse's station, but I couldn't. I clenched the arm of the chair, and another stabbing pain impaled my chest.

Blackness.

I slowly began to wake up. I was in a hospital bed, and a nurse was injecting something into the IV in my arm.

Why am I in a hospital bed? How did I get here?

Questions answered themselves as the day's events began to form in my mind.

The night before had been happy. Jared had come home excited about a leaf raking activity he had organized in our neighborhood with his fellow fourteen-year-old scouts. They were to start the service activity at our house this morning, so their seven rakes leaned against the front fence.

It was early November, but a small heat wave had left many fall leaves still clinging to the trees. The ground was still free of snow. The weather was chilling rapidly and needed leaf raking's were anticipated. Jared happily came home and reported that he had two more people signed up for his other scout project, getting people to be organ donors. He now had a total of twelve.

Maisie spent her evening with friends talking about her project helping the local animal shelter get more pets into homes. Recently, she adopted two guinea pigs, a black short-haired named Ozzie, and a brown and white long-haired named Lucy. She and two of her friends fed, played, and groomed them before returning the cuties to their newly cleaned boxes.

A snowstorm alert interrupted my favorite TV show.

True to the report, the storm furiously rolled in about midnight, accompanied by raging winds. Heavy drifts piled up against the house, burying everything, including the leaf rakes.

My neighborhood was established in the 1940s. It was heavily landscaped with young elm seedlings. Years later, they became huge overgrown giant trees taking over the park strips between the sidewalk and the streets and were rarely maintained by the municipality. The night of the storm was frightful as we could hear them cracking, and I wondered if the limbs would break. We all finally fell asleep.

A loud crash brought me out of a sound sleep around even o'clock the next morning. Before I could get out of bed, I heard another crash. I stumbled, threw off my nightgown, and grabbed a shirt and a pair of pants. While pulling on my shoes, I noticed an awful smell that seemed to come from the basement.

Maisie's and Jared's rooms were down there, and I ran down the stairs. When I reached the bottom, I looked in the laundry room on my right. I had left clothes on the dryer, and they were still there, but eerie blue flames were on the wall behind them. It looked like a gas heater flame, but it covered the entire block wall. Nothing else was burning.

Puzzled, I stepped through the narrow door into the laundry room, and just as I did, the room exploded. The blast threw me backward out of the room, scorching my clothes, and singeing off six inches of my hair.

I scrambled to my feet and screamed at Maisie and Jared to get out.

The hall was on fire, and I couldn't get Jared's door open. I ran in, pulled Maisie out of her bed, and pushed her past the burning hall while still screaming at Jared. But he didn't answer.

The entire house was an inferno, and my lungs were filling with burning toxic smoke. I fell to the floor as two firemen came down what was left of the stairs. One of them stood me up and pulled me outside to safety.

I saw other firemen dressed in protective gear rush into the house carrying a stretcher. When they brought Jared out, he was unconscious. They loaded his stretcher into the back of an ambulance and rushed to the nearest hospital. My neighbor Melanie helped Maisie and me into her car and followed them.

When we got to the hospital, Jared had been taken into the emergency room. Maisie, Melanie, and I found chairs in the waiting room. Twenty minutes went by before an ER doctor came out and told us that Jared had died.

Maisie started crying and shaking uncontrollably, and I wrapped my arms around her. A nurse hurried out to speak to us. She indicated that they found a pulse, and Jared was now hooked up to a mechanical ventilator, and they were doing other life support procedures. Several doctors were attending to him and had no answers at that time.

We just sat there waiting. More waiting and praying for a different result.

Friends and family began arriving to lend us their support. My brother, John, came with my sister-in-law, Anne. She sat with Maisie, offering comfort, and talking with her.

I felt sick, and everything started to blur. I woke up in a hospital bed. Since I had breathed in toxic fumes, I was suffering from cyanide poisoning. The danger is a coma, lung injury, seizures, and death. They treated me with antidotes, amyl nitrite, and then sodium nitrite intravenously.

Cyanide ions interfere with cellular respiration, causing the body's tissues not to be able to use oxygen. Nitrates widen the arteries and veins to improve the blood flow, allowing more oxygen-rich blood to reach the heart muscle; they had reached *me* in time. The antidotes worked, and I was released.

My neighbor, Melanie, had taken Maisie home to her house.

Jared had been moved to a private room in the emergency department. I walked in to see him surrounded with medical equipment, and I could hardly see his face behind the ventilator. The sight of him in that condition was appalling. My heart was breaking, and I felt a terrible physical pain. My boy's life was being drained out of him. He was too damaged, and there was no antidote that could help him. His heart was damaged, and his lungs could not function without the ventilator. He was in a coma.

I leaned over and kissed his forehead and gently touched his hair. My tears dripped onto his cheeks as I held his hand. I sat in the chair beside his bed and laid my head as close as I could get to him.

Exhausted, I fell asleep.

It was late when my friend Melanie came and picked me up. I didn't know how to leave him; I couldn't let go. One of the nurses took my hand and gently slipped Jared's out of it. She said, "You should go now. I'll be here with him all night."

Melanie put her arm around me, and we walked out of his room through what seemed like an endless corridor to get outside. A misty haze had formed around the light posts, and deep snow edged the freshly plowed sidewalks. A stark gloominess seemed to envelope both of us, producing an unusual surrealistic environment.

Nothing looked or felt real.

As we walked, Melanie said, "Kathy, there's something that I need to tell you before we leave. Your house has," she paused and then continued in a quivering voice. "Well, you'll see it tomorrow, but…" she paused again. "Well, the condition of your house…it's not good."

I stopped walking and froze with an emotionless stare. "How bad is it?"

Turning toward me, she placed her hands on my shoulders and said, "Kathy, it burned to the ground. The firefighters flooded it to put out the flames. What didn't burn up was ruined by water. They couldn't save it. Your house is completely destroyed."

I felt like I had been kicked in the stomach. I doubled over and sat down on the cold sidewalk. My children were homeless. But what did a house matter? My son was dying.

I pounded the concrete with my fists. The pain and the darkness were eating me alive, and I put my head to the ground and screamed.

"I love him so much! This can't be happening! I just want to take my kids and go home! Please God, make it stop!" I crumbled into a heap of despair.

Melanie grabbed my hands, holding them as still as she could.

"Look at me. Kathy, look at me!"

I raised my tear-soaked face and stared at her.

"You need to listen to me. Maisie is with my daughter, waiting for you. She needs her mother right now. She is counting on you and doesn't need to see you like this. Jared doesn't want you to be like this either. They love you. We all love you, so please just stand up and go with me to the car, okay?"

Melanie stood, extended her hand, and pulled me to my feet.

CHAPTER 13

The Decision

WHEN I ARRIVED AT THE HOSPITAL early the next morning, Jared's condition had not changed. The lead neurologist told me Jared had only a minute amount of brain activity. The pulmonary specialist told me they had taken his ventilator off for twelve minutes while supplying oxygenated blood through his veins. There had been no response from his lungs. The cardiologist confirmed that his heart was only operating through artificial means, confirming for me that I alone had the authority to turn off the life support machines.

I left the empty treatment room where we had been talking and sat alone in a corner of the emergency waiting room.

Suddenly, everything was organized chaos. I heard the medical helicopter land on the emergency pad of the hospital roof. The speaker announced it was bringing in a sixteen-year-old male that had been accidentally shot in the chest.

The hospital staff immediately went into emergency procedure mode, each one concisely fulfilling their duties as expediently as possible. The blood-soaked victim was rolled quickly through the hall on a gurney. They passed me, while doctors shouted, he was headed for surgery in the ER. I watched when his parents arrived during all the turmoil and were pushed aside. The doors to the ER abruptly closed in front of their faces. Obviously panicked and afraid, the grief-stricken parents found their way to the waiting room chairs near me. Through the conversation between the two of them, I learned their son had been with friends in a different city, and his parents had been notified he was being flown here for treatment.

One hour and fifteen minutes passed. The parents were moved into a curtained treatment bay, only separated from me by a thin beige fabric. I wasn't trying to eavesdrop, but I couldn't help but overhear.

The doctor said, "I am sorry, we used every procedure available to save your son's life. The surgery was unsuccessful."

"What do you mean unsuccessful?" The mother sounded desperate.

"I deeply regret having to tell you both that your son has passed away."

Her voice escalated. "No, he has not. You must be wrong. That can't be true!"

I sat transfixed to my chair. A lump formed in my throat as I knew the pain that was coming next.

"We did every procedure available to help him, but the damage to his chest was too extensive. His vital organs…"

Her desperation changed to anger. "No! I don't want to hear what you couldn't do. I want to hear what you are going to do now!"

I felt such sadness and empathy for her. I knew these terrifying feelings that had been my constant companions for over the past two days.

The doctor quietly said, "I'm truly sorry, you're free to wait here while they finish preparing your son. A medical assistant will come for you when he is ready, so you can see him if you like. We can offer you help through Hospital Social Services. Ask at the nurse's station if that is something you would like. Before I leave, is there anything else that you would like to ask?"

"No, I don't want any of your social services. I want for to you stop being stupid and wasting time. I want you to get back in there and help my son."

"Marsha, stop. Let him go." Her husband tried to comfort her.

How many worlds have been destroyed in this room?

I could hear Marsha sobbing.

I felt sorry for her, and yet I had a fleeting moment of jealousy. In my reality, I had a terrifying decision to make, one that she had been spared from. I stood and went to Jared's room. His face was no longer covered. His head was being supported by a chinrest, and he was still hooked up to multiple machines. No one else was in his room.

I ran my fingers through his hair; he looked so still. The damage to him was very apparent. Even if he could possibly live, what kind of life would he have. I took his hand in mine. It was warm and pliable.

"I love you so very much," I whispered. "I'm so sorry this happened to you."

I bent down and kissed his forehead. "I have something to tell you, Jared, and I hope you can hear me. I don't want you to live and be trapped in a broken body. I know that you're worried about me and Maisie, and that you might stay here because of us. Don't you do that. If you have a chance to go where it's a wonderful place, you go. Don't look back, just go. We'll be fine, and we'll be with you on the other side soon enough. We love you so very much and always will."

As I spoke to him, tears began streaming down his face and filling up his chinrest. I grabbed two tissues and began wiping his cheeks. More tears came. I cleared them away until the two tissues were soaked.

The neurologist came in, and I suppose seeing me crying, he asked, "Kathleen, are you alright?"

I answered him with a question, "May I ask you something?"

"Yes, of course."

"Can Jared cry?"

"No, he can't. He doesn't have that capability anymore. All you will ever see is a slight glint of moisture in the corners of his eyes where we administer eye drops. You'll never see more than that."

"Thank you for explaining that to me."

He left the room.

I was still holding the tear-soaked tissues, and I looked up. "Thank you, God, for letting me know that he heard me."

CHAPTER 14

The Gift

I HAD TRIED to get a good night's sleep, but I just couldn't. My mind was still swimming in uncertain muck. I still had that terrible decision to deal with, and I had spent most of the night on my knees praying for help. I got dressed and woke Maisie. I told her in detail what the doctors had said to me and asked her to come with me to the hospital. We got there at nine o'clock.

Jared was having more tests run, so Maisie and I waited in his room. She shared her feelings with me and bravely supported whatever decision I made. I could sense the terrible pain inside her.

When the nurses brought Jared back, he was different from yesterday. The color of his face had changed from pink to a sallow gray. I touched his hand, and it was cold.

"Mom, I don't think Jared is in there anymore."

I looked at Maisie and nodded sadly. She was right. He was gone.

"Mom, Jared doesn't want his body to stay like that. I know that somehow you feel guilty about letting him go. But you have to do it. He would want you to." She poked him and began to cry. "I love him, too, but see he's not there. Mom, that's just not him."

Putting her arms around me, we both sobbed. We cried until we had no tears left. I wiped my face off and then hers. Reluctantly, I knew she was right.

"Let's go find the doctor and tell him that we have made our decision." Holding each other by the hand, we left his room.

We met with two of his doctors and told them what we had decided. The neurologist told us what to expect next with Jared. Emotionally exhausted, we walked to the waiting room where a thin young blonde lady warmly greeted us.

"Hello. My name is Sally Baird. I'm with Intermountain Organ Recovery. May I speak with you? We can sit over here if you like."

Maisie and I followed her to a quiet corner of the waiting room. Sally began explaining to us about the possibility of Jared becoming an organ donor. I detected a nervousness in her voice as she carefully and thoughtfully presented her case. We found out later that most people were very hesitant and knew very little about organ donation at that time. Most people declined having a loved one be a donor.

I looked at Maisie, and she nodded.

"Yes."

Sally looked almost speechless. "Are you certain?"

"Yes, we are," added Maisie. "My brother's scout project is about signing up organ donors. He really believes in it. He signed up twelve people already and signed himself up, too."

Sally's eyes began to tear up. "What a wonderful gift that he decided to do that. He sounds like an amazing young man."

Tears streamed down my face, and I wiped them away. "He is. I do have a request. We do not want his body to be used for medical research. We want the donations to go to local people who are in need by no fault of their own. Also, we are going to have a blessing of release. That's a special prayer to dedicate his soul to God. We need to notify our family that we will have that done tonight. Afterward, they can do the organ procedures."

"Thank you. Words cannot express the immense joy of the recipients. We have so many people on our waiting list." She handed me a clipboard. "I have some papers for you to sign, and then our board will meet and contact the selected individuals."

I signed the release and handed it back to her.

Sally smiled. "The procedures will all take place tonight. God bless you both for this generous gift."

CHAPTER 15

Calm After the Storm

I CALLED MY BROTHER JOHN to let him know of our decision. I asked him to say the blessing of release. He felt honored to do it and offered to arrange the event.

Two days later, Jared's viewing was held at the Lanier Mortuary. It was heavily attended as we received much support from our church and community. Schoolmates and personnel from Maisie's and Jared's school also came. When we arrived with our immediate family, there was a line of people outside for two city blocks, and more were arriving. We had a family prayer, then Maisie and I were shown where to stand in the room with Jared's casket. The noise and crowd were overwhelming. Lanier representatives did their best to calm the noise down. We stood for several hours talking to people who had come to pay their respects and were touched by all their support, but it was exhausting.

Then something happened we could never be prepared

for. Words of unkindness, criticism, and religious doctrines began to emerge. A lot of those comments were from people we didn't even know.

One such comment was hurled at us. "Why didn't you get him out? Why did you leave him in the house to die?"

Other comments included, "The news said that Jared was suspected of being in a street gang and they burned your house down. Is that true?" The sad fact was the city newspaper did print that story on their front page. They retracted it two weeks later with a one liner on the back page.

Then there were those who thought that they were helping to leave an important message in the form of a mini sermon or a religious one liner. "Jared will be fine. He is with God now."

Or "God doesn't give you any trial you can't make it through."

And finally, "You were brave in the pre-existence. You knew this would happen, and you chose to be his mother anyway. We are confident that you can overcome this."

My plastic smile began to fade. A minister I had never met was there. He asked me if I had been saved yet and handed me a pamphlet with his name and address on it. Other probably well-meaning people began leaving things. One was the statue of a mother and son. The bestower of this gift told me that it had been passed around at other funerals to mothers that had sons who died. I was the sixth mother to receive it. She encouraged me to keep it for a while and then find another bereaved mother to give it to.

I did see people that knew us well that didn't preach to me. They just offered us hugs and tears which we really appreciated.

To the other responses, I wanted to say, *If you truly know us, you know that we already have a wonderful testimony of God and His son, Jesus Christ, but please let us grieve. Do you not see my dead son in the casket? Do you not see the terrible grief of his sister?*

It finally became too much for me. The fatigue finally overwhelmed me. I stumbled and nearly fainted. My brother, John, saw the difficulty I was in. He rushed to catch me, escorted me out of the room, and gave me a glass of water. He gave me a quick hug, and then left to take my place in line.

The day after Jared's funeral, I went to face the condition of my home. I had been advised not to go in because of the dangerous conditions there, but I needed to see it once for myself. The doctors informed me that Jared had lost consciousness and did not wake up again. They said he had not experienced any pain, and that he did not have any burns on him. I still needed to know for myself.

Wearing a face mask, I went through what was left of the front door. The sight was deplorable. I had been told that the living room was the least affected, but it was shocking. The intense heat had melted everything. The rapid cooling of the fire hoses had instantly stopped the motion of melting. Things were now frozen at that exact moment in time. I was enveloped in an eerie surrealistic domain. The clock on the wall, while dripping, had frozen, still reflecting a sense of movement. In its ghostly state, it manifested the exact time the house had died as 7:42.

A beloved family painting still clung to the wall. The center had disintegrated leaving one small remnant with a portion of Jared's face. My grand piano stood like a silent stoic giant. Its once beautiful walnut finish was now bubbled and covered with layers of ashes and debris. The open lid revealed broken mangled strings. I walked into the kitchen and stared at a melted blob that had once been my refrigerator. I tripped on another melted blob that I discovered later was my iron. The fire department asked for permission to keep it for demonstration purposes.

I walked to the basement stairs. Now I knew why I was told to stay out of the house. The appalling sight was black, dark, and burned. I knew it was unsafe, but I stepped down, I had to see Jared's room. The floor crunched with each step I took. When I reached his room, I found the door shut. The hall was very narrow and most likely the firemen, after bringing Jared out, had to shut it to get enough room to negotiate the stairs.

I opened the door. Light was streaming in from a small broken window. His room was exactly the same as the last time I was in there. His green leather coat was still draped over his desk chair. Nothing had burned.

I continued down the hall to Maisie's room with tears

streaming down my face. I noticed the hall rafters were charred. I opened her bedroom door, and from another broken window, there was enough light to see the room clearly. Her room had burned, and the bed was charred leaving nothing of the bedding but floating flakes. Layers of gray soot covered the walls. I felt a terrible shocking sensation as it became so apparent that Maisie had narrowly escaped being burned alive.

The sliding doors to one closet were closed. This room had once been my bedroom, and when I taught the adult Sunday School class at my church, I often made my own posters and visual aids. I kept them in this closet.

I slowly opened it. The belongings inside were dirty and dark but had been somewhat protected by the lack of oxygen, I guess from the doors being shut. A large gray rectangle caught my eye. It was a piece of posterboard pressed tightly against the wall. I carefully peeled it off. The side toward me had darkened from the intense heat, but the side facing the wall was still white and perfect. It read, "For as in Adam all die, even so in Christ shall all be made alive."

I took the poster and Jared's jacket with me to the backyard. I sat in Jared's favorite outdoor chair, and I cried, releasing so many of my feelings. In the middle of what seemed like only darkness and despair, I knew these words were true.

CHAPTER 16

The Owl

A LITTLE OVER FOUR YEARS PASSED. Maisie was grown and married, and I met and married Gary. With our baby Robbie, we moved to Alaska.

It was a cold winter morning in our mountain home in Bear Valley, Alaska. Deep, freshly fallen snow covered our two acres of spruce forested land that connected to the Chugach National Forest. Gary, our son Robbie, and I lived at the southern end of Anchorage where the Seward Highway headed past the Turn-again Arm toward Seward, on the Kenai Peninsula. When you turn left off Seward onto Rabbit Creek Road and continue past Homestead Park, you find yourself driving into the mountains. Oftentimes you would drive through misty clouds breaking through into the beautiful Bear Valley surrounded by more alpine giants.

The land could be a beautiful mystical backdrop for a charming fairy tale. Our forest was always teeming with many different animals including black bears, moose, porcupines, and lynx. A family of ermine had taken up residency in our wood pile.

The sky was also full of life and splendor, frequently revealing eagles, raptors, and great white owls. Once, we were under the flight path of two giant Siberian Steller's Sea eagles, rarely seen, one of which had been spotted while flying over a remote native village. A local Piper Cub pilot flew near the immense bird. He promptly radioed the local villages to quickly move their children inside for protection.

Strategically perched, my home provided a perfect view of the entire valley dramatically sloping downward where melting snow created Rabbit Creek. The bright moon reflected off the fresh endless snow, enveloping the dark green spruce trees with a layered white essence. The brightness lit up hazy clouds, edging them with white light contrasting against the deep navy-blue sky. It was a mesmerizing sight.

A frosty chill filled the air on one extraordinary night, when all was silent, and the clear sky displayed wavy green curtains of the dancing northern lights. I stood in my large family room gazing at the sky from the two giant picture windows designed to capture this exact amazing view.

I moved closer, pressing myself against the glass. As I looked upward, I saw it! What was coming down from over my roof directly in front of me? If there had been no glass, I could have touched it. I saw two huge legs and feet with talons curved backward like a human's arms bent at the elbows with hands curved bearing huge claws. I was looking at its underbelly. As it descended further down in front of me, the size of its immense wings spanned the entire length of the room. It glided further out, gracefully catching the moonlight on its white, angel-like feathers.

A giant snowy owl artfully sailed without a ripple toward the moon. I felt my heart pounding as I had nearly forgotten to breathe. It was one of the most beautiful of God's creations that I had ever seen. Tears streamed down my face, its image not only etched into my mind, but the awe and wonderment burned deeply into my soul.

CHAPTER 17

The Light

THIS OCTOBER MORNING, having readied myself and prewarmed my SUV, I planned to visit an elderly friend. Before Gary left for work at the army base, he had thoughtfully plowed the driveway of our two-and-a-half-acre property. I cautiously drove out onto the road.

Wow, the sky is really clear after so much snow last night. No one has plowed the road yet. I'm glad Gary left me the Suburban.

I turned left and started my descent down Nickleen Street. I drove slowly as I was familiar with the road becoming glaciated and forming thick layers of ice.

I felt the tires slide a little. "Whoa, this could get really nasty," I said out loud.

Bear Valley was not part of the municipality of Anchorage, and the roads were not publicly maintained.

At the end of Nickleen, I needed to turn left, pass the mailboxes, and then turn right onto Height's Hill. If I failed to make the left turn, I could end up nose down in Rabbit Creek.

Still talking out loud, I said, "Okay, it's time to be very careful. Turn slowly around this corner."

I was barely moving when I made the turn because I had driven this country road for years. But I didn't realize that I had slowed down too much for the weight of the vehicle, it was as if I was caught in slow motion. My car began sliding to the right, catching me completely off guard. My right front tire dropped my SUV into a newly dug ten-foot-deep drainage ditch.

My SUV rolled and flipped upside down, into the freezing Rabbit Creek, blocking the water like a dam. I couldn't get the doors open because both front doors were jammed by the embankment. Freezing icy water was coming through the cracks in the windows, and it was getting dark inside.

My seat belt was holding me upside down like a bat, and I couldn't breathe. Frantically, I struggled to unbuckle my belt and fell into the freezing cold water. The side windows were now completely immersed, and I realized the car was upside down. I was stuck and couldn't get past the seats to get out!

It was bitter cold, and I knew I would die from hypothermia before I would drown. I only had a couple of minutes before I wouldn't be able to think.

The SUV was tilted, so if I could get to the back, I might have more air. Frantically, I began to search for a way out.

My mind was racing. *This really might be it. I might really die! I can't die here on our street by the mailboxes!*

Gary and Robbie won't be able to live here anymore. They will have to pass where I died every day!

Please Father, let me know what to do!

A calmness came over me, and in my mind I heard, *Remember you are upside down. You need to push the back of the middle seat up. Go under the water, through the space, and go toward the light.* Then the message repeated. *Push up with all your might and go toward the light.*

I reached over and found the edge of the middle seat which was now completely submerged. I pushed up as hard as I could until the space between the seat and the ceiling was now wide enough for me to go through. I pushed up until my head cleared the water, and I gasped a big gulp of fresh air. I could see that the back doors were also jammed against the embankment, and the back window was broken. The back end of the SUV was higher than the front.

I put my drenched sweater around my right leg and kicked the rest of the window out. I squeezed between the car and the snow-covered bank, until I was able to climb out and stand on the bottom of the car. But it was much lower than the road. I clawed through the snow, by grabbing shoots of the alders, and pulled myself up until I was faced down on the road.

Freezing and exhausted, I walked to the corner of Nickleen Street. My neighbor Sandra lived up the hill, about a half a block away. She was an emergency room nurse and rarely at home.

I couldn't think anymore, and my lungs ached, but I started walking toward it. I saw two people standing in her driveway, but they were blurry, and I stopped.

I heard Sandra yell, "Are you alright?"

"Car wreck!" I screamed and collapsed.

I woke up in a warm hospital bed with stitches in my leg. I later found out that Sandra's brother had carried me to her home where she administered first aid and called an ambulance.

I will never forget that day, when a calm spirit instructed me to, *Push up with all your might and go toward the light.*

These dear words have helped me throughout my life. My spirit knows their source. More trials have come and will continue to come, but I am no longer lost and afraid.

CHAPTER 18

Farewell to Grandma Evie

THE END OF EARTHLY TIME comes for all of us. After a long and wonderful life, our dear Grandma Evie died at ninety-four. She was a devout Catholic woman of Polish ancestry who had spent her life dedicated to her religion and helping others. Her kind heart had earned her the love of many. When she died, she wanted to be transported to Michigan and buried in the plot next to Albert, her beloved husband.

But her son, Duncan, who was my former husband, shared none of her attributes.

Because she suffered from glaucoma and had lost most of her vision, Duncan had unfortunately convinced Evie to add his name to her bank account, so he could assist her in paying her bills. It only took two years for Duncan to withdraw all her funds. The money she had put aside for her funeral expense was gone, leaving only her meager insurance policy. Duncan hurriedly had her cremated and arranged a small Catholic mass for her. It was followed by a little get-together in the church cafeteria where punch and cookies were served by a few of Duncan's acquaintances.

Our daughter, Maisie, arranged a few pictures from Grandma's life for a display in the church foyer. She purchased two large fresh floral arrangements of red roses and white lilies. She asked Duncan to purchase more floral arrangements, but he declined. His excuse was the priest advised having a large display to be inappropriate.

Maisie felt that Grandma should have gotten a better send-off where more friends and family could remember and honor her. She wanted to have a nice memorial event for Grandma Evie at her house. After the mass, I approached Duncan with Maisie's request to have Evie's urn at her home for the weekend. To my surprise, he granted her request and let me take the urn for the next three days.

Many extended family and friends came to honor Grandma. My brother and two sisters came with several of their children and grandchildren. Maisie had arranged her dining room table with the flowers and the display from the church. Several of her cousins had already arrived and were busy placing food on the kitchen counters.

Gary and I brought Evie and arrived Saturday at noon.

Maisie greeted us at the door. "Come on in. Here, let me take Grandma."

I handed her the beautiful blue floral urn. She smiled and carefully cradled it.

"This time Grandma won't have any difficulty walking up the stairs. She will be able to hear better, too, and not feel so left out." She smiled as a glint of tears formed in her eyes.

We headed up the split-level entry through the living room to the connecting dining room.

Maisie placed Grandma Evie on the marble table by a large bouquet of flowers. "I got her favorite roses, aren't they pretty? I thought she would like them."

"I'm sure she does and appreciates your thoughtfulness." I gave her a little hug, picked up a white napkin, and blotted the tears from her eyes.

"Mom, I just couldn't stand it that Dad didn't plan anything for her. Sometimes, he makes me so angry. He didn't even buy any flowers. He said the church didn't want anything set up in the foyer. That wasn't true. He just didn't want to pay for anything. I talked to her priest, and he's the one who let us set up a nice display of pictures and some flowers, otherwise, there wouldn't have been anything for her."

"I know, Maisie, he always makes everything difficult. Try not to let it ruin this beautiful memorial you planned. Grandma Evie loves you very much. She always told everybody that she had only one granddaughter, but she got the best one anyone could ever hope for. You also gave her two beautiful great granddaughters who are the joy of her heart."

I hugged her shoulders. "Okay now, what can I do to help you get the food ready?"

People began arriving, and soon the house filled with tender conversations of fond memories about Grandma Evie. More food found its way to the table.

My niece Amy arrived with an armload of food and put a large package of rolls on the table. "Oh, Maisie, those flowers are beautiful. If I remember right, those are Evie's favorite flowers."

"Yes, she loves roses, especially red ones."

"They are very beautiful. That's a neat looking cloisonné jar. I love the blue flowers and delicate leaves. The little white flowers are pretty, too." Amy examined it more closely. "It's interesting. It looks kind of like an urn."

Not all the guests were aware that I had been able to get approval to bring Evie to our gathering.

"It is an urn," said Maisie. "That's Grandma."

"Oh no, I'm so sorry!" Amy hurried to move the rolls that were leaning against the urn. "I didn't mean to covered her up!"

"That's alright," laughed Maisie. "Grandma loves rolls, and I see that you brought her favorite kind."

Maisie rearranged the table and placed a small decorative pedestal under the urn. "This will keep her up higher out of the food."

Everyone enjoyed the delicious meal as more fond stories of Grandma Evie were shared while sounds of happy children playing filled the cozy home.

My granddaughter, Chloe, who was seven, and six-year-old great-niece Kelly, were getting chocolate chip cookies from the kitchen. They paused in deep contemplation to study the urn.

After a moment of silence, Kelly asked, "Chloe, is Grandma Evie really in there?"

"Yep, she is," Chloe said with a serious firm nod.

Another moment of silence passed.

"How did they get her in there?" asked Kelly.

Chloe shook her head. "I don't know, but I know she's in there."

Another moment passed as they gave the urn another serious stare.

"Okay, Chloe, can we go play in your room now?"

"Sure, let's go."

Both girls gently patted the top of the urn and said in unison, "Bye, Grandma."

They hurried off, giggling as they went.

CHAPTER 19

Dead Cleaning

WHAT IS DEAD CLEANING? It simply is downsizing and cleaning your house, so your kids don't have to do it after you die. Some professionals call this process by a more genteel name, but it is still dead cleaning. There are many reasons why people keep stuff. The list is almost as numerous as the excess of things one keeps. For me, I needed to have a clean organized home as soon as possible. It was the top priority on my bucket list.

The most difficult decision was resolving what was essential to keep. What did I really need? I knew I would be happier if my house was in order. It would be so much easier to maintain, and I would have more time to do other things. I didn't want to stay in the trap of keeping something because it was still in good condition, would make a good gift, or reminded me of some special time or someone.

I felt guilty for getting rid of some things. I could over-think my plan, make too many lists, or try to do too much and drown myself in the process. I also needed to give myself permission to keep a few important sentimental items, while still reminding myself that it was alright to let some of those things go, and I was not betraying the memory of someone by doing so.

I knew it was possible to achieve my goal in a short time because I had done this before.

The phone rang, and when I answered, it was my brother.

"Hello, Kathy, this is John."

"Well, hello, how are you doing? It's been a while since we have talked."

"I know. I was thinking about how long it's been since we've seen each other, and I got this idea. I have decided to sell the Hobbs house. I've been making trips there to get it ready to put on the market. I need to go again next month, and I thought that you might like to go with me. I could get you a shuttle ticket from Salt Lake City to Cedar City, and then we could take the van and drive to Hobbs. I think you would enjoy it, and I could use your help. We could see our old stomping grounds again. On the way back, we could go through Arizona and visit our cousins. We could see Aunt Nellie, she's in her nineties now. It would be good to see her again. We would be gone for about three weeks. I'd love for you to go."

"That would be fun. We rarely get to spend any time

together. It's been years since I've been to Hobbs, and I would like to see it again. I'll run it past Gary and let you know."

"Anne says to give our love to him. I'll talk to you soon."

Gary encouraged me to go. He said it would be good for me to spend time with family and see my childhood home again. He was right. I had precious hidden memories anxious to be part of my life again. It was as if I was going to find them in an archaeological dig.

CHAPTER 20

The Unexpected Surprise

JOHN AND I FINALLY REACHED HOBBS. After checking into our motel, we drove to our childhood home. We moved from Hobbs to Artesia when I was in the fifth grade. The last time I went to our family home, I was thirty-five years old. At that time, I was sixty-seven. A sinking feeling came over me as John drove into the driveway.

The house and property were completely unrecognizable. The white paint had weathered away, exposing dingy gray streaks of bare wood. Parts of our old home were sinking from years of wind and rain. The foundation was eroded causing the floor to sink as much as eighteen inches in some places. Drought had also frequented New Mexico for the last decade, killing most of the vegetation. Overgrown dead trees and bushes lay strewn around the entire acre.

I got out of the car and stood motionless, trying to reconstruct a scene from my memory. I imagined a comfortable three-bedroom white house with dark green trim appearing. I pictured beautiful white, yellow, and purple irises edging the now missing white wooden fence. I heard our black and white English setter, Suzy, barking as she ran to greet me. A loud whinny echoed in my head as I imagined Rowdy, my brown Shetland pony, racing through the property. When he saw me, he tossed his light-yellow mane and kicked up his heels with delight. He was six weeks old when I got him on my seventh birthday. He was tiny enough to ride home with me in the back seat of our Buick.

My father had worked as a welder for a judge who owned a nearby ranch. Dad couldn't afford the asking price for the pony, so the judge let him exchange work for Rowdy.

John unlocked the front door. I left my imagination and followed him inside. An unbelievable shock hit me like a brick. I froze. The plaster ceilings had leaked, and portions were caving in, leaving debris on the now water-stained hardwood floors. Light fixtures were in disrepair. I could not comprehend the full extent of the damage as the view was blocked by heaps of stuff from the last renter who had been hoarding items for years. I tripped around stacked barrels in an attempt to find the hall. Struggling to find a place to stand, I bumped into a box and spilled its contents of used cottage cheese containers on what little clear floor space remained. Kicking through it, I squeezed my way down the hall to the childhood bedroom I had shared with my older sister, Jean. I struggled to open the door, but it would not budge. I shoved as hard as I could, moving it inward by only about four inches. I peered inside to see boxes, clutter, and furniture stacked precariously from the floor to the ceiling. There was no way to enter. All the other rooms of the house were in the same condition.

We went back to the front yard to open the door to the attached garage. My father had built this massive structure tall enough for his motorhome and long enough to park three vehicles. Another shocking sight revealed more discarded materials heaped as high as the ceiling. Boxes of junk, old furniture, stoves, refrigerators, and more large items made up the first level. On top were mounds of old flattened boxes that once held large televisions, vacuums, and other large appliances. There were old sewing machines, unusable small appliances, dishes, boxes of old clothing, cans of food, and old tools everywhere.

The structure had been invaded by rodents and foxes. The body of a dehydrated fox was still in there. The smell was stifling. John explained that the municipality had recently built a city disposal and recycling center, but prior to that, neighborhood residents had to travel to another city to dispose of their waste materials, and the fees were very expensive.

There were other major repairs to make to the house including fixing a caving in foundation on the south side. We only had five days to accomplish this feat. There was a small rusty trailer that my father had made years ago from the bed of a pickup truck. The plan was to use it to haul away the mass.

Previous longtime tenants of the house had allowed friends and neighbors to store unwanted trash in there. Eventually, the third layer became a free garbage dump stuffed so full of things that we could not walk inside the door. John's goal was to clear a path wide enough to drive a truck and trailer through the garage to the door on the other side.

On his last visit, John had cut down the trees in the backyard, and the city had issued a violation warning because it had not been cleaned up. Once we reached the backyard, we would take care of it. The alternative would have been to remove the wooden fence and enter the backyard from the street, leaving the property at risk for vandals.

CHAPTER 21

Two Glass Reindeer

JOHN WANTED TO TAKE ME on a tour of Hobbs to visit a few places from our past before we began the projects. First, we went to see a small house that our father had built when John was a baby. My father had received employment as a welder from Ohio Oil Company. He was offered housing as part of his benefits. When he and my mother arrived at the camp, they were surprised to learn that the promised small shotgun-like house had not been built yet. My dad received permission to build a small dwelling on the lot that was reserved for him. Using pieces of plywood, he built a shed-like structure with simple hand tools. Eventually, when the camp house was ready, Dad sold his handmade house. The new owner moved it to his property and eventually added more rooms. The exterior was now painted bright red. The small structure was still someone's home, and a well-kept flowerbed adorned the front.

We paused across the street to reminisce for a few minutes, then John drove us to another location.

We traveled a short distance west to an industrial part of town. A few older buildings lined the street. We turned left and saw a railroad crossing bordered by a gravel road. John pulled over and parked on a neighboring gravel lot by the tracks.

"Do you know where you are?" asked John.

"No, I don't recognize this place at all."

"That's probably because the last time you were here, you were only three years old. It was Christmas time in 1957. Where we are parked, there used to be a small shack. A man built it out of pallets for his wife and three children. Our sister, Jean, went to school with his daughter. They were in the second grade together."

"I do have a faint memory of that Christmas. I remember our family giving toys out to children on the street. It was dark because Mom handed some cap guns to a boy. The package was clear plastic, and they looked shiny when he held them by the head lights of our car."

"That's right," said John with a pleasant nod. "Do you remember the little glass reindeer that Mom had?"

"Yes, I remember them. They are red and about two inches high. Mom kept them on the divider shelf between our kitchen and our living room for years. They weren't really reindeer. Jean just called them that because we got them at Christmas time. One has antlers, and the other one has white spots on its back. That one has a broken leg, and

Jean still has them. I do remember Mom telling the story of how she got them. I just don't remember being there."

"Well, you were there, and you are there now. This is the exact spot where the shack was. I remember it well." John paused in deep thought. After a few minutes, he began to recall the memory.

"One day, Jean came home from school feeling sad. It was right before the Christmas holidays, and the kids at school were talking at recess about what they wanted for Christmas. Jean said that one of her classmates, Jenny, was quietly sitting alone on the steps. She asked her what was wrong, and Jenny told her that her family wasn't getting anything for Christmas. Jean assured her that Santa would probably come. Jenny cried and told Jean that he wouldn't because her parents didn't have any money to leave for him. Jenny's favorite part of Christmas was when her family made paper ornaments together and decorated the tree. She said that this year they couldn't have a tree."

I was familiar with this story, but I had never heard John tell it before. It was very touching to hear the tenderness in his voice as he recalled it after so many years.

"Well, you can guess what Mom did after having been raised by a single, widowed mother. She and Dad got busy trying to figure out a way to stretch their budget to provide Christmas for this family, too. Mom and Dad fixed up two old bikes for Jenny and her brother, Tim. The bikes needed new balloon tires, so they went to see Dad's friend, Frank, who owned a local White's store to see if he could give them a good price. When Frank found out what they were doing, he gave them the tires for free. Frank told Dad that he would have to pay employees overtime to get the store's inventory finished by the end of the year. He said that if they wanted to help needy children, he would furnish the toys and do a tax write off instead of doing the inventory."

John continued, "On Christmas Eve, we came here first. I helped Dad take a small evergreen tree to the door, and then we took the bikes. Jean brought two dolls from the White's store, Mom carried food and stockings full of candy. You followed along holding the plastic star for the top of the tree. Little Jenny answered the door, and soon the sounds of Christmas excitement filled the tiny house. The children were wide-eyed and thrilled with the presents. Their parents were filled with gratitude. Jenny's mother wanted to give a gift to our mom. She took two little glass reindeer off a tiny shelf. With tears in her eyes, she handed them to Mom and gave her a hug. We exchanged happy tidings and then left to go back to the White's store where Frank was waiting for us. He filled the large trunk of our old Buick with toys. That night he loaded it three times. It was the best Christmas ever."

We both sat in silence for several minutes. Then John started the van.

"Okay, Kathy, we have one more place to go before lunch."

I was curious. "Where's that?"

"It's a surprise. Let's see how fast you can recognize it."

CHAPTER 22

Two Pebbles

JOHN DROVE CLOSER to the Hobbs house through a more suburban area. The scenery began to look familiar. We passed the city park that was lovely and green like a desert oasis. He drove through another subdivision and parked in front of an elementary school. Even though it had been remodeled and added onto over the years, I recognized the school immediately. I came here as a child. It was summer now, and the school was closed.

"You can get out and look around if you like. I'll wait here."

"Thanks. I would like to take a look around. I won't be very long."

I opened the door and stepped out onto the sidewalk that was next to the bus lane. It ran parallel to the school all the way back to the playground. I walked past the place where Mrs. Cartwright always parked her bus after school. In my mind, I could hear busy students hurrying to board the bus. She always greeted me in a pleasant voice and with a smile.

I continued walking until I reached the playground. The end of the school was to my right. It still had the same concrete entryway with three steps where I used to line up after recess. I paused and sat down on the top step. Memories of being a seven-year-old second grader began flooding my mind. I imagined the sound of Mrs. Weger's whistle blowing.

Alright children, it's time to line up and go to lunch.

My thoughts reverted to a day in school.

The upper grades went to lunch first. The lower grades went to lunch after a fifteen-minute recess. Students could buy lunch or bring one from home. On the way to the cafeteria, I got my cartoon lunch pail and three pennies from my cubby to buy a carton of milk. Today, my special treat was a bag of potato chips. I took my place in line.

Entering the cafeteria, we took our assigned places at table number three. The benches and tables were unfolded and rolled out from the wall. The girls sat on one side and the boys on the other. Across the table from me sat Juan, a shy boy who didn't speak very often. He opened his lunch sack and took out his usual two slices of bread with only a thin piece of bologna between them. My lunch consisted of a tuna sandwich, a homemade chocolate chip cookie, and instead of my usual apple slices, I had a bag of potato chips. Having given my three cents to Mrs. Weger, a carton of milk was handed to me.

I watched Juan hungrily eat his sandwich. He didn't get any milk. I was still eating as he sat quietly watching me.

"Mrs. Weger told us to finish our lunches that we'll be going back to class in five minutes."

I looked at Juan. I quickly pushed my bag of potato chips toward him. He hurriedly took the bag and put it in his well-used paper sack.

One day, I asked Juan where he lived before he moved here. He said he lived in a lot of different places with his mom and dad. They used to live in Mexico with his cousins and grandparents, but now he was sad because he didn't get to see them anymore. I asked him if that was why he knew how to speak Spanish. He told me that everyone in his family spoke Spanish, but none of them spoke English, so his dad sent him to school to learn it.

When I asked him why they had to move so much, he told me that his parents worked on farms. After everything was picked, they would have to move to find more work. They were migrant workers. I asked him when he thought they would have to move again. He said he didn't know, but they usually only stayed somewhere for a couple of months, and they had already been here a month. I felt bad for him. I wouldn't want to always have to move around.

Juan always had a sad look on his face. At recess, he always had two pebbles in his pocket. He would take them out, look at them, and roll them around in his hand. One day, I asked him if they were special rocks because he always had them and played with them a lot. He asked me if I wanted to look at them, and he let me hold them. The two stones were gray and smooth. They felt soft when I ran my fingers over them. I knew they were the kind of rocks that had been smoothed by water.

I asked him about that, and he said yes that he got them at a river. The big one between here and Mexico. He told me they got to our country by swimming through the river and that was really hard and terrible. The water was deep and fast, and his dad had to hold onto him tight and hold him up to get air. He looked frightened when he was telling me, and his voice started to shake.

Then he started to cry. He took a deep breath, bit onto his lip, and wiped his face off with his sleeve. He said his mom was swimming with his little sister, and the water was very strong. His sister's head kept going under the water. His dad got Juan out of the water and went back to help them. When he pulled his sister out of the water, she wasn't breathing. He laid her down on the ground and tried hard, but he couldn't get her to breathe. His mom started to cry. Some other people came to help, but nothing worked. They picked her up and took her away, and where she was lying, Juan found those two pebbles. That's all he had left of her.

His face was wet from crying, so I wiped it off with my scarf. I gave the rocks back to him then the bell rang, and we went back to class. It was Friday, and after school when I got on the bus, I saw Juan's father pick him up.

Monday came, and Juan was not at school. But then on Thursday he came back. We sat together at recess.

He told me that he wouldn't be at school anymore. I asked him why, and he told me that his parents had picked all the crops, and his dad got other work, so they had to leave again. I asked him where he was going, and he said somewhere better where his mom and dad could work longer. He told me he wouldn't get to see me anymore. I started to cry, so I held my breath so I wouldn't make any noise. Juan reached into his pocket and took out one of his pebbles. He placed it in my hand and told me to take it, and whenever I held it, to think about him. He said I was his friend, and he would always be my friend, too.

The last bell rang. Juan's father came to pick him up and check him out of school. I gathered my things and headed to the school bus. As I got in line, Juan hurried over and gave me a big hug, then he turned and disappeared into the crowd of students.

I felt a warm hand on my shoulder. I turned and stood up from the step.

"Are you ready to go?" asked John. "I need to stop at the hardware store, and we should probably eat lunch before that. Where would you like to eat?"

"Oh, anywhere would be fine."

"I know this great Mexican restaurant that is my favorite place to eat at when I come to Hobbs."

"Sounds good to me."

CHAPTER 23

Delay Tactics

J OHN WORKED for several companies via the Internet. He had planned to take time off, but emergencies kept him working all the next morning at the hotel. We were only about a five-minute drive from the house. I offered to go over and start doing something. He was uneasy about me starting without him, so after lunch, we went together to reassess the situation.

My brother had assumed the responsibility of the house and property after my father died. It originally had been a small house in an oil company's community for employees. When that community disbanded, my father purchased the tiny house and put it on an acre of land. John was twelve years old at the time. He helped my dad and was with him for every part of the relocation from the foundation to eventually adding new rooms. He grew up in that house until his last year of high school when our father's job transferred him to a nearby city. John served in the Air Force and retired as a Lieutenant Colonel before starting his present profession in which he has also been very successful. During that time, he had lived considerable distances from the house and had not been able to monitor it or care for it as he would have liked. Keeping it rented was difficult in a small New Mexico town. He felt fortunate to have it occupied to prevent it from being vandalized. Now we stood staring at the daunting task ahead of us.

"Well, Kathy, I think that we should bring several boxes at a time out here with the dollies and sort things into different piles. One for things we want to keep, another for things we can donate, another pile for the valuable items, and of course a pile to take to the trash. I think that we need a water-vac, so we can wash down the cement and vacuum up the muddy water. I need to go to the hardware store for some other things, so we'll get one there. I want a battery-operated one so I can use it later for more portable jobs."

"Okay, and while we are out, let's get some food and drinks for here, so we can work without having to stop."

"That's a good idea."

We drove to the hardware store. I planned on a quick trip but realized that a lot of materials were needed for the foundation repairs under the house. The selection of these items took a lot of time. Finally, John started looking at water vacuums. He was focusing on the battery-operated types, but they had a lot smaller capacity than the regular ones. He kept comparing several, contemplating out loud just which one was the best.

"Are you sure that you really want to get a water-vac. We use them quite a bit at home, and I think that we have way too much dirt in the garage for one to be very effective."

"No, I'm sure." He stood there another ten minutes just looking.

I tried again. "You know that Gary and I have a five gallon one and a ten gallon one. These are only two gallons. They also use filters that the bigger ones don't always need."

He just kept looking at them. More time went by.

He picked up the smaller battery-operated model. "Well, I think I will get this one."

Earlier, at one glance I had observed just inside the garage door enough dirt to fill up a trash barrel. I had reservations about John thinking the job would be easier by flooding the garage and attempting to water-vac it out. I was imaging thick deep mud clogging a two-gallon battery-operated machine.

"Okay, but you might want to get a bigger one for the garage. I think that it would be a good idea to sweep out as much dirt as we can first."

He reached over and picked up the five-gallon model.

"I'm ready to go. Here, you can take the keys and wait for me in the van and that way you won't have to stand in line while I check out."

Great idea.

I thanked him as he handed me the keys.

John remained in the store for quite some time. He came out and spent another twenty minutes installing the connection for a temporary mini trailer he had been fashioning. We went to the house, dropped off the supplies, and returned to our motel.

Now I was really confused. We had used up an entire day and never started to clean out the garage. Something was not quite right. Later that evening, we went out to eat at one of his favorite Mexican restaurants. He began reminiscing about our parents and when we lived there as children. Being five years older than me, he could share a lot of things that I had been too little to know or remember. John talked a lot about our dad and his relationship with him at that age.

When my brother assumed responsibility for the Hobbs house, he did not want to sell it. In future years, it had become a burden to him. He lived too far away to properly maintain it. Needed repairs were very expensive. There were issues with the well, and the roof needed new shingles. Whenever John had time off from his job, he and his wife, Anne, were constantly working on the house. It was a big relief when he finally decided to get the house ready to sell. One of the problems was that we were still dealing with COVID and found that it was nearly impossible to hire any extra help.

John enthusiastically pointed to the menu items. "This is my favorite Mexican restaurant, at least in Hobbs. Isn't this great? I recommend these side dishes. If you'd like, we can order several and share them."

"That's fine with me. I'm sure that I will enjoy any of them. Go ahead and order for me, too."

The server came and took our order. This was one of those rare times that John could sit and leisurely talk.

"Tomorrow, I have another Zoom meeting. I'm afraid that we will get a late start again. I need to go under the house and pour two concrete footings to put the jacks on. Each one can support six thousand pounds of weight. When I tighten the jacks, that should raise the floor, and give it enough support."

"You know, John, you could drop me off before your nine o'clock meeting, and I could get a start in the garage. I hate to just sit around when I could be helping."

"No, I don't want you to be over there by yourself. I think it would be better if we went together."

The server placed various dishes of food delights on the table.

"Oh, this looks great."

"John, we're running out of time. At least let me go start making a path. I promise not to throw anything in the trash trailer until you get there. I could at least pull out a few boxes and sweep up part of the floor. I have my cell phone if anything happens. It's only five minutes away."

"Well, let me think about it. Let's eat this yummy food."

We enjoyed our delicious meal as John continued reminiscing. He recalled memories of the camp where we had originally lived. It was as though his whole childhood was unfolding in his head. He told me stories that I had never heard before. We laughed and talked as I began to understand. To him, this house was all he had left of Mom and Dad. Despite its condition, he was having a terrible time letting it go. There, John could always be that twelve-year-old boy with his dad. He was also attached to the memories of his best friend. They grew up together, attended the same schools, and went to scouts. Luke called us his second family. He became my other big brother, and we even went to a year of college together. Later, he and his family lived in the house for years and raised a daughter there. Sadness came when Luke became ill with a debilitating disease.

CHAPTER 24

The Nemesis

THE NEXT MORNING after breakfast, John took me to the house, so I could start working on the garage while he completed a project for his employer.

I opened the garage door. It was truly intimidating. John had purchased a pull cart that I immediately started loading. My goal was to move enough stuff to be able to stand inside for a better assessment. I moved load after load onto the driveway. Finally, I was able to clear a path six feet long and four feet wide. Using a flashlight, I peered further into the garage and could see more things. It was like an archaeological dig. Each layer, heavily covered with dirt, represented the time period in which it was stored. Out-of-date sewing machines, folded into their cases next to an old blonde wooden console television, served as the foundation for the next layer of old stereo equipment where their cabinets substituted as shelves for the next layer of boxes. I swept up piles of dirt before taking a break to investigate what I had set aside.

The boxes were full of old clothes from different decades. Some were filled with large bedding, others were full of household items such as lamps, dishes, plates, and the like. Later, I found boxes full of old church manuals, tablecloths, and scout supplies. Out-of-date boxes of dehydrated food in number ten size cans had exploded from years of summer heat. Another box held sewing supplies. John informed me that when the small church down the street was enlarged and renovated, church leaders stored supplies in the garage. I don't think he realized they never moved them back to the church. There had been considerable flooding at one time, probably years ago, and most of the boxes I opened were damaged. But now they were dry, misshapen, and stained. I could see nothing worth keeping or even worthy of being placed in the donation pile. I just left the boxes in the driveway, hoping that John would agree to trash them all.

At 12:30 p.m., John arrived with the van.

"Hi, I stopped off and got us some fried chicken meals." He cheerfully handed me a box. "Those chairs by the porch are out of the sun, let's sit there. I see that you haven't done any sorting yet. I can help you for a little while before I work on the foundation."

"About those boxes," I said before biting off another bite of juicy chicken. "They're in really bad shape. A lot of things are damaged and not worth keeping at this point. I think many things need to be thrown away."

"Let's finish eating then we can take a look."

Another twenty minutes went by before John decided to examine the pile.

"Kathy, did you see this set of dishes over here?"

"Yes, there are some broken ones and are no longer a complete set. They're quite dirty."

"Let's put them over here in the donate pile. Here's a box of Jennifer's clothes. I bet she would like to have these."

The pile of donation boxes was rapidly growing.

"John, do you know of any place in Hobbs that will pick these up, especially on short notice? We only have a few days."

"Probably. Let's set them over here for now."

Soon we relocated to the crawl space under the house. We needed to clear it out, put in concrete footings, and install the jacks. Using hand wenches, chains, and help from the van, we managed to pull out two old water tanks. It must have been easier to leave them under the house than to remove them when the tanks were replaced. Once again, there was no more time that day to clean the garage. Before we left, I could see the frustration on John's face. This garage was his nemesis. Even if there were things worth saving, there was no place to put them. He lived two states away, would have to rent a truck to remove the items, and then he would need to rent several storage sheds. John didn't have enough time or manpower. We only had three days to finish.

I put my hand on his shoulder. "Come on, let's go. It's getting dark."

We went back to John's favorite Mexican food place. I could see why he liked it so much. The restaurant was very charming and had true Mexican décor, with white high walls like a mission. A water fountain graced the central plaza, and colorful hand-painted wooden parrots on swings hung from the ceiling. The servers wore authentic costumes, and the food was delicious.

I decided to address the glaring issue head on.

"John, we're going to run out of time. We don't need to go over every item in every box."

"I realize that. I *am* aware." He was irritated. "But we need to check everything carefully. There are probably some good things that we want to keep mixed in with the trash. We don't want to throw anything important away, especially if someone else could use it."

The problem was that everything John saw today was something important. We didn't throw anything away. Every item was a cherished thing, even if he had never seen it before. It was Mom's or Dad's, a belonging of a precious friend, related to memory, or from the church he had gone to as a youth. Somehow, John was connected to it. If he got rid of anything, it was as if in some way, he was being disloyal to them.

For me, I had not been there for so many years, that all my attachments were broken, and new ones had never formed. I could look at all the things objectively and see only their monetary value. My challenge was how to help John see the items the same way.

"John, in the morning while you're at your meeting, I'll load the trailer with trash. I promise to go through everything before throwing anything away. There is a lot of obvious trash that I can take care of first. You can check through the trailer before it goes to the dump."

"Okay, see what you can do."

We got a good night's rest.

The next morning, John drove me to the house. I immediately went into action. My goal for the morning was to clear a large notable free space in the garage. I needed to completely load the trailer, so it would be ready to take to the dump when John arrived. My hope was that if he could see significant progress, he would let me continue in that direction. In the next three hours, I completely cleared a space about the size of a car. I found a few things that I carefully set aside in a medium box for his approval. To me, they weren't worth keeping, but I wanted to show him that I had been looking through every box. I swept out another garbage bag full of dirt. John pulled into the driveway.

"Wow, are you kidding me? You really got a lot done this morning."

For the first time, I saw some relief in his face.

"I found a few things that you may like to go through. I put them over here in this box. The trailer is ready to take to the dump whenever you want to hitch it up."

"Let me look." He leaned over and surveyed its content. "Looks great. I'll hitch it up, and we can go."

I tried not to look shocked. "Alright, I'm ready."

That afternoon we took two more trailer loads to the dump. I worked on getting things out of the garage as John worked under the house on the foundation. I was now finding heavier items. Over the next day, it took us both to lift some things into the trailer. Upon the discovery of some possibly usable items in slightly better condition, John began to relapse and slow down the cleaning process. I uncovered an old stereo cabinet with a glass door front and open back. It held numerous coffee cans filled with miscellaneous items such as screwdrivers, hammers, and other small tools. I grabbed some rags, intending to block the back so the items would not spill out when we lifted it into the trailer. I covered the cabinet with an old sheet in case the glass door broke. When we loaded it into the trailer, it slipped backward, spilling some of the contents.

John removed the sheet. "Look, Kathy! There are tools inside. We need to go through this again."

Instinctively, I grabbed hold of his hands and held them down. "No, John, no."

"But Kathy, these are tools. Maybe some were Dad's."

"No, these were stored a lot later, so they can't be Dad's. You already have a lot of tools. The van is already full, and you have nowhere to store them when you get home," I reminded him with a quiet but firm voice while still holding his hands.

He gave me a cute boyish look. "Can I just have one?"

I rolled my eyes. "Well, I guess so." I laughed and released his hands.

He smiled and held up a ball-peen hammer. "I'll take this one."

CHAPTER 25

Enlightenment

OVER THE NEXT COUPLE OF DAYS, we were able to completely empty the garage. By extending our stay by one more day, we were able to find an after-hours company to take away the heavy furniture and appliances. One of the last things to go was the original stove our mother had used before I started to school.

Suddenly my four-year-old self was standing on a green speckled kitchen chair and carefully stirring a pot of pineapple filling. My mother was teaching me how to make a pineapple upside down cake. The smell was wonderful. The cake would be ready and waiting for John and my sister, Jean, when they got off the school bus.

The noise of the trash removal company loading it for recycling brought me back to the present. A lump formed in my throat as tears filled my eyes. It was like someone was trying to take away a precious memory forever, but they couldn't. That cherished memory was in my stewardship, and I would always keep it safe. Now I understood that John had the same pain for almost every item. He had carried that anguish for years. I walked over and took his hand as we watched the last load drive away until it was no longer in sight.

John hugged my shoulders. "Well, Kath, we did it. It is finally done."

"Yep, Bubby, we sure did."

We both chuckled at the mention of his nickname.

Over the next week, we finished our trip through the Southwest, stopping to see relatives along the way. We had a wonderful time sharing many memories that we experienced together and many we had not. We learned a lot more about each other. We renewed our common interests. We both play the trumpet, and we each own several. We often talk about the different models we have, what particular things we like about each one, and what different qualities they have.

My son Jared also played the trumpet. One year for Christmas, I gave him a silver Stradivarius model. I was a single working mom and saved for a long time to buy it. This trumpet became his pride and joy. After my divorce when Jared's father walked out of his life, John stepped up as a father figure, going on scout trips with him, band concerts, and vacations. He was always there for him, and John was very close to Jared. He went through a very difficult time when Jared died, and I gave John his trumpet. He still has it.

As a child, I remember going with my mother to take John to Mr. Miller's house for his trumpet lessons. A lesson was thirty minutes long, so we just waited in the car for him. I could hear the wonderful trumpets as they played Bach duets. I decided that I wanted to be a trumpeter just like my big brother. I loved saying the word *trumpeter.*

When I started the sixth grade, I was eligible to enroll in band. I asked my parents for permission to join. My father said I could as long as I used a school instrument, because they could not afford to buy a trumpet for me.

Soon, using a school instrument became problematic as it was old and not well maintained. One day my father brought home a trumpet he had purchased from a second-hand store. It needed some work, had a few dents, and a damaged valve. His plan was to repair it for me in his welding shop. The repairs turned out to be more difficult than he anticipated, and the trumpet remained in his shop having never reached its potential.

While we were in Hobbs, John found the trumpet still on the shelf in Dad's shop. John painstakingly had it completely restored to its original state. A year later, with much love and pride, he gave it to me for my birthday. As I enjoy playing it, I'm reminded of my father's and my brother's love for me.

CHAPTER 26

The Ocean

A COOL BREEZE enveloped us as my sister Lavender, my niece Mary, and I climbed out of the truck and headed toward the sandy beach. The welcoming sights, sounds, and smell of the salty ocean filled our senses with awe. Seagulls squawked over our heads as they flew down from the grayish blue skies to land on the seashore. The gathering flock was intermittently separated by delicate sandpipers scurrying among the gulls in search of food. As one bird flew away, another would take its place. I stared at the mesmerizing waves that rolled in one after another as the ocean replenished itself. A wave that had begun its existence further out to sea as a huge, white, and powerful billow, began to calm and reduce in power as it neared the end of its cycle, caressing the shoreline in front of me, sometimes depositing shells as the living sea gave up its treasures.

"Kathy, would you like a beach chair? I brought three," offered Lavender.

"I would, thank you." I took one from her arm and unfolded it on the sand. "It's truly beautiful here. I have really missed the ocean."

I sat down and inhaled a long slow breath of the pure oxygenated air. I exhaled slowly as Mary unfolded her beach chair and joined us.

Mary smiled. "We thought you would enjoy this particular beach, it's our favorite spot. We always bring our family and friends here when they come to visit. Sometimes, we come early to collect the larger shells before the tourist shops make their rounds. They sell a lot of them."

"It's beautiful and peaceful here. I'm glad we got to come. I've been looking forward to it."

I scanned the beach, taking in all the sights. The clouds were pierced by glistening rays of sunlight that sparkled on the waves, and a cool wind flowed gently through my platinum hair. The last time I was here, it had been golden blonde and a foot longer. The sights and sounds were now triggering my memories, causing them to surface and flow to the front edges of my mind just like the endless sea as it directed waves to the edges of the sand.

A young couple arrived, laughing as they got out of their car. A pretty girl reached for the hand of a handsome young man. Instead of taking it, he picked her up and carried her near the water's edge. She giggled as he set her down. Taking her by the hand, they strolled down the beach. The wind left a trail of long blonde hair behind her until it was caught by his muscular arm when he placed it around her shoulders.

She stopped to pick up a seashell. She handed it to him, he examined it, then stuffed it in his pocket. He took her hand, and they resumed walking down the beach until they became small silhouettes.

My mind rushed back in time.

It had been fifty years since I had been to this beach, yet the memories were still vivid and bright like the sea itself.

Aaron had retrieved a large shell and placed it in my hand.

Wow, that's a pretty one. I told him. Not as pretty as you are. He had winked at me. I had laughed. Oh sure, not today. I'm covered with sand, and my hair is a mess.

He told me he loved my messy blonde hair, and the sand in it. I told him that I loved his wavy brown hair. I teased him and rubbed his head with my sandy hand. He grabbed me around the waist and tickled my sides. I told him to stop and managed to grab another handful of sand and threw it at him.

Our play fight landed us flat on the beach. Aaron placed his arm under my head. We looked up at what seemed like a magical sky full of wonderful birds, and fairytale sounds.

"Aunt Kathy, Mom is getting our lunch out of the truck. What would you like to drink?" asked Mary. "We have orange juice, lemonade, and bottled water."

"I'll have water."

"It's a bit breezy now. Would you like me to get your jacket for you?"

"Yes, that would be nice. Thank you."

Aaron, I never got to tell you goodbye. Here I am nearly seventy years old, and you have been gone for fifty years of that. I still remember the sound of your voice, the cute winks that you would give me with those beautiful blue eyes, and how it felt to run my fingers through your soft curly brown hair.

I sighed as Mary returned with my jacket.

"Are you alright?" Mary looked concerned.

"Oh, I'm just remembering the last time that I was here."

"I didn't realize you had been here before. When was that?"

"When I was a young college girl. Did I ever tell you about Aaron?"

"No, I don't think you ever mentioned him before."

"Well, he was the love of my life, when I was nineteen that is."

"How did you meet him?"

"I met him in my first year of college. I was a shy freshman, and he was a dashing sophomore. I saw him in the music building while he was getting into his locker near the student lounge. I was in there writing my English assignment."

Mary grinned. "Sounds exciting, what did he look like?"

"He was handsome, about six feet tall, with dark brown curly hair, and crystal sea-blue eyes. He had one of those smiles that could melt any girl, and he knew it, too." I chuckled just thinking about it.

"He sounds really cute."

"Every day, right after lunch, Aaron would go to his locker. I admit that I started intentionally going to the music lounge and sitting in a chair where he could see me, and pretended to be writing an assignment.

"One day, Aaron opened his locker, turned in my direction, and just stood there staring at me. His silence was impacting my ability to write my paper more than the loud, noisy students who had just been released from their classes. I hurriedly looked down to give the impression that I was diligently working. After a minute or two, I glanced up, and he was still watching me. I pretended to ignore him as a nervous lump formed in my throat. I wasn't sure which was speeding up more, how fast I was writing or the rate of my heartbeat. He closed his locker and made his way through the surge of busy students and sat down in the chair next to me.

"He told me I was going to hurt my hand if I didn't stop writing and look up once in a while. He leaned over, eyed my paper, and pretended to read. Twas a dark and dreary night as the hungry formidable beast stalked its injured prey. Opening its terrifying mouth…

"I laughed and told him that's not what it says.

"He just kept going in a high-pitched voice. Oh, please kind sir, don't eat me. I'm only a small bitter morsel. If you don't eat me, I will show you a much bigger, tastier meal. He was so funny, and he won my heart."

"What was he talking about?"

"He was just messing around. Let me see if I can relate it in his words. He changed his voice to a low scary tone. Alright then, show me where this bigger, tastier meal is. Do it now, or you're a goner. Then he changed his voice again, it's over there, kind sir. See its tail lying in the mud by that giant rock. Then he said, Yes, I do see it!

"Without even breaking character he said, suddenly, the giant rock rose up, opened its huge mouth, and devoured Terrifying Mouth."

Mary was laughing now, and I continued to be Aaron in a more pleasant voice. "Thank you, Little Bitter Morsel. I hadn't eaten in days. At this point he changed his voice again. You are most welcome. Can I go for a ride on your back now? Sure, Little Bitter Morsel. Hold on tight. I feel like flying.

"Aaron handed my paper back to me, and I burst out laughing.

"He looked so pleased with himself and said, there, I finished your paper for you, so how about we go to lunch? I hear the cafeteria might be serving Terrifying Mouth for lunch.

"I told him that would be great. He took my hand and

helped me out of the chair and then walked me all the way to the cafeteria."

I stared at the water totally lost in thought.

Mary poked my arm. "And?"

I smiled. "From that day on, we were nearly inseparable. The next semester we took several of the same classes together. He was a vocal major, and I was a piano major. We performed together many times."

"Aunt Kathy, did your relationship with Aaron ever become very serious?"

"Oh yes, it did. Serious enough that he asked me to marry him."

"If you were engaged, how come you have never mentioned him before now?" Mary looked puzzled. "At least I don't remember you ever talking about him before."

"Well, that's because earlier in my life, talking about him was always very difficult. Then as the years went by, I pushed the painful memories away. As my life went on, I put new memories in the front of my mind to lessen the frequency of the old memories coming back. That helped dull the pain. As more years went by, my suffering seemed to dissipate. It's strange how being here today has renewed those memories in great detail as if only yesterday I had been here with him."

I took a deep breath and slowly exhaled to keep my composure. I could feel the pressure of tears in my eyes waiting to escape. A few finally did.

"Oh, how silly of me." I searched my pocket for a

tissue. "That young couple that just passed reminded me how much Aaron and I loved each other. We planned to spend our whole lives together."

"I don't think you're being silly. Can I ask you, for two people that loved each other so much, what happened?"

I took another deep breath. I allowed my mind to travel back in time again. It was as if I was standing in front of a large weathered wooden door with a rusty metal lock on it. Around my neck, I was still wearing a golden chain with the key that would unlock it. As I opened the door and stepped through it, I began recounting the memory to Mary.

CHAPTER 27

The Memory

"SUMMER VACATION had finally come. Aaron and I decided to spend two weeks at his parents' home in Corpus Christi, Texas. After that, I planned to go home and see my parents for two weeks and then meet Aaron back at Eastern New Mexico University for an additional two weeks before the fall semester started. We both had work study grants.

"We flew into the small Corpus Christi airport and were greeted by his parents, Bob and Susan Renner. Aaron greeted his tiny mother with a bear hug that nearly picked her up off the ground. I was surprised by her tiny delicate stature, straight shoulder-length red hair, and green eyes. Aaron looked nothing like her. His father greeted him with a warm embrace and a few pats on the back. He was a large husky-built man who towered over his wife. He had short dark speckled grey hair, brown eyes, and a dark complexion. This also surprised me as Aaron did not resemble him either. I later found out that Aaron was an adopted only child.

"We had a great two weeks in Corpus. We came here to this beach several times where we didn't have a care in the world. We enjoyed our break from school. His parents were very accommodating, warm hearted, and easy to get along with.

"The last time we were here, Aaron's mother packed a special picnic lunch for us. I noticed that Aaron was acting just a bit differently from his usual jovial self, almost like he was a bit nervous or something. He was deep in thought as we held hands and walked along the beach. I broke the silence to try to bring a smile to his serious face.

"I asked him how he was going to manage being away from me for the next two weeks? I told him I didn't want him to die of loneliness. Then I kissed his cheek, purposely leaving a lipstick print on it. He said I missed and gave me a long romantic kiss.

"I caught my breath, and then still with that deeply serious look on his face, he kissed me again. He pulled me down, and we sat on the sand. He put his arms around me, and we sat quietly watching the waves. Being with him felt so right. He was my best friend, my love, and all I wanted in a companion. I knew that he felt the same way about me. For a while, time seemed to stand still just for us. Finally, he said, Kathy, you know that I love you, and I believe that you love me, too. I know that we talked about finishing school first, but that seems so far away. I can wait that long if I know you are really committed to spending the rest of your life with me. He reached into his pocket and pulled out a tiny black box and opened it. Inside was a gold ring displaying a tiny shimmering diamond in the center. He took my left hand and placed it on my ring finger. He softly kissed my hand, looked into my eyes, and said, Kathy, I love you. Will you marry me?

"Well, I started to cry when I said yes. He lifted my chin and began wiping my tears away, and asked me if it was that bad to say yes? I didn't think asking would make you cry. I was hoping for a happier, more enthusiastic response. I told him I am happy and gave him another kiss.

"He pulled me to my feet and said we'd better go tell his parents because his mom had been waiting all day to hear my answer. He told me his parents really liked me. We held hands and walked one more time along the beach. I felt so happy and alive. I heard every sound, saw every lovely thing, felt every breeze, and the magical touch of Aaron's hand in mine."

I looked directly at Mary. "This was the beauty of being young and in love."

By this time Lavender had joined us and had sat on the other side of me.

"The next day, we attended church with his mom and dad. They proudly introduced me to everyone as Aaron's fiancée. After church, we visited with his pastor. He shared his delight about our engagement. After church, we called my parents and told them about our engagement. They were also very happy about our news. My parents had met Aaron when they came to one of our recitals at the university. They were only a three-hour drive away. Aaron couldn't go home with me because he was helping his father in his auto body shop for the next two weeks.

"Monday morning, Aaron drove me to the airport. We said our goodbyes and promised to call each other. In those days, we didn't have cell phones, just phones usually attached to the wall with a long cord. Calling long distance was also expensive. We agreed to limit our calls to short ones and only a couple of times a week. I called him when I got to my parents' house to let him know that I had arrived safely. We said our I love you's, and he promised to call me in a couple of days.

"Wednesday, bright and early, Aaron called. He told me that he missed me but was glad for the time he had there to help his dad. We talked briefly about our work study programs and our arrival times back at school. We said our goodbyes, and I promised to call him on Friday. He told me I better make it Saturday, as he was going with his dad to pick up some auto parts in a neighboring town.

"I enjoyed spending time with my parents. It was fun being with my mom and talking about my future plans with Aaron. We spent some of our time repainting the living room a lovely creamy color. We installed a new hanging corner lamp she had gotten with several books of Gold Bond stamps. It had tangerine colored glass and an orange tassel on a pull chain that contrasted nicely with their popular avocado carpet. My father, who was an artist part time when he wasn't working for an oil company, had finished a beautiful oil painting of a New Mexico sunset that we hung above their bright floral sofa.

"Saturday morning came, and I excitedly made my phone call to Aaron at the designated time. I called and anxiously waited for him to answer. The phone just kept ringing. In those days, we didn't have answering machines, and there was no way to leave a message. I let it ring several times. I hung up, waited five minutes, and then called again. There was still no answer. I reasoned that it was Saturday, and they probably went somewhere. I tried calling again around five. I was disappointed, so I resumed helping my mom with a few other projects.

"About four o'clock, we began preparing dinner. We made my dad's favorite chicken enchiladas. It was now five thirty, so I thought it would be a good time to call Aaron again. I waited anxiously as I heard the phone ring. There still was no answer. I waited patiently as it rang over ten times. I hung up and called again. All it did was ring. I wondered why someone didn't answer the phone and decided maybe they all went somewhere. Something probably came up, and Aaron just isn't home yet. I bet he will call me back soon. I kept rationalizing.

"Over the next week, I kept calling, but I could never reach anyone. I had this sinking, terrible feeling inside of me. I couldn't figure out what was happening and why he hadn't called. I remember looking down at my ring and twirling it around my finger. Maybe he had changed his mind? Maybe his parents really did not approve of me, and that's why they were not answering the phone? Maybe they went out of town to visit somebody. I knew he had two uncles. One is divorced and lives in Cleveland, and the other uncle is elderly and lives in a retirement facility in Tulsa, Oklahoma. They wouldn't have gone there either." I leaned my elbows on my knees. "I was coming up with all kinds of reasons I hadn't heard from him, and I kept nervously twisting my ring until my finger hurt. I couldn't get it out of my head that maybe something terrible had happened to them.

"A couple of days drug by, and finally, I was on a Greyhound bus back to Eastern. I arrived back at my dorm around five o'clock. It was still two weeks before the fall term officially started. The campus was still fairly empty. The cafeteria and buildings were open for students as well as faculty members who were returning for work studies and other pre-semester activities. Aaron and I were both expected to sign in on Tuesday morning at nine o'clock in the main music building office to receive our work study schedules and assignments. I got there at eight thirty a.m. and waited in the lobby, hoping to see Aaron when he arrived. Students and faculty began filling the building. He never came. I finally went into the office. I was directed to the large hall to begin my training. The day went by and still no Aaron. I hurried back to my dorm.

Individual rooms had no phones. Each of the three floors had a phone, but long-distance calling was not allowed. The dorm lobby had two pay phones, but they were currently in use by returning students calling home. Tired and worried, I went to my room to rest awhile until a phone would be available. Exhausted, I fell asleep and did not wake up until early the next morning.

"I woke up and looked at the time. It was six thirty. It was probably a good time to call again as most students were still asleep. Since I had fallen asleep in my clothes, I grabbed my wallet and hurried downstairs to the phones. It now had been two-and-a-half weeks since I had seen Aaron and two weeks since our last phone call. I hurriedly put coins into the phone and called his number. To my horror, I got a message that said, We're sorry. The number you are calling is no longer in service. I hung up. The coins clanked as they returned to the change compartment. I frantically grabbed them out, nearly dropping them as I put them back into the slot to try the call again. For a second time, the message began to repeat itself. In anger, I slammed down the receiver. I ran back upstairs to my room, threw myself on the bed, and sobbed. My body ached, and my heart was racing. I became nauseated and made my way to the toilet, but because I hadn't eaten the night before, I had nothing in my stomach to throw up. I sprawled out onto the cold bathroom floor. After twenty minutes, I got up and took a shower. The warm water helped my tired body but could do nothing for my aching heart. In a zombie-like state, I dressed, dried my hair, applied a small amount of makeup, and made it to my work study training.

"Another week went by, and Aaron still did not come. Returning students filled the campus. My roommate arrived as well as old friends, many asking me where Aaron was. I simply said that I didn't know. A few saw my engagement ring and were baffled by my answer. Fall classes were back in session, and it now had been a month since I had any contact with him. I knew in my heart that he was not coming back and resigned myself to my situation. I was heartsick.

"When I came back from classes, there was a message for me at the desk. It was a request from my bishop to see me. I called the number he left and made an appointment to see him the next evening at six o'clock. I entered the church and took a seat outside his office. I was surprised when my roommate came in and sat down beside me.

"I asked her if she had an appointment with the bishop, too. She said she did, that it was right after mine. I told her she could go first, but she said she wasn't in any hurry.

"Bishop Anderson opened his office door, greeted us, and invited me to come in.

"He asked me how I was doing and if I got enrolled in all the courses I wanted to take. He seemed to be making small talk about my scholarship and work study.

"Then Bishop Anderson paused, cupped his hands together, and leaned forward with his elbows on his desk.

His happy demeanor changed, and a pensive look replaced his smile, and he sounded nervous. He said, well, I'm sure you are wondering why I have asked you to be here. I could hear the tension in his voice. He gave a long silent pause, and I knew that something was not quite right.

"I tried to joke and asked him if it was a new calling, was it really that bad. When he said no with an attempt at a smile, he had a painful look on his face. Then he said it's not a new calling but that he had something very difficult to tell me. He said he had prayed and prayed for the right words. He finally said he had received a call the day before from Pastor John Green. My heart began to race because I recognized the name of Aaron's pastor. I met him when I attended church with him in Corpus Christi.

"Then he told me that a few weeks ago, Aaron and his parents were in a car accident. I didn't get it, and I asked how bad it was, and if they were alright. I was starting to panic. He told me that on a Friday evening, his family was coming back from visiting friends, they were hit by a drunk driver. They were rushed by ambulance to Corpus Christi Regional Hospital. His father died upon arrival. His mother died later that same evening. Aaron was in an unconscious state and passed away twenty-four hours later."

Mary was staring at me. "My gosh, Aunt Kathy, I'm so sorry."

"Yeah, it was horrible. I sobbed. Bishop Anderson quickly stood and opened the door and Janey and her boyfriend, Casey, came in. They all stayed with me until I calmed down and was able to breathe more calmly. I figured out why Janey was really there.

"I found out later that Aaron's uncle from Cleveland had settled all the family's affairs. After the funeral was held, as he was cleaning out the house, he found a letter that Aaron had written to me but not posted yet. It contained information about our engagement and Aaron's love for me. It had my address on it. He gave it to Pastor Green who remembered that I was in an LDS ward at Eastern and was able to contact my bishop. Later, I received Aaron's letter from Pastor Green."

Mary asked, "I can't even imagine. What did you do?"

"Well, I withdrew from the university and went home to my parents. After a year, I enrolled at Brigham Young University in Utah, changed my major, and started a new life." I shrugged. "Yeah, that's what I did."

After finishing my memory of Aaron with Mary and Lavender, we sat quietly enjoying the beauty and wonderment of our surroundings. A calm peaceful feeling enveloped me. I was happy to be in this magnificent place again. Fifty years had gone by without having Aaron in my life, but during those fifty years, I had a full and complete life. I had children and grandchildren with my dear husband, Gary. I also have a large extended family. My brother's and two sisters' families have given me many nieces and nephews. I had many accomplishments and adventures. Those years were packed with living.

The sun was now lower in the sky, and the cool breeze was now transforming into a chilly wind. Lavender began packing up the picnic items. It was time for us to go. Mary folded up our chairs, and we headed for the truck. Halfway there, I turned around for one last look at this beloved spot and to hear the sounds calling to me for one last time. The fresh air against my face, pulse of the ocean, and graceful sailing birds made me feel so alive. I gently placed two fingers against my lips and sent a loving kiss toward the thriving sea and whispered,

"Goodbye, Aaron."

CHAPTER 28

Jared's Well

LOVE MY LIFE! I love each ray of sunshine, every drop of rain, and even the snowflakes that tingle as they melt against my face. I am grateful for every moment of happiness that I have ever been blessed with. I learned to appreciate each moment of sorrow, grief, and pain. While in those moments, I discovered who I really was as my weaknesses changed to strengths and my doubts transformed into faith. Just like the seeds I planted in my garden; I have struggled to reach up out of the cold darkness and find the Master's warm light.

In my past, I was often afraid of things yet to come. Now I anxiously rush toward the new day, grateful for its arrival, and enjoy anticipating what it has in store for me. I've learned to find joy, harvesting it like the produce in my vegetable garden. Sometimes, I must wait for happy moments to come as they also require nurturing, patience, and time to grow.

I love to inhale the clean air after a gentle spring rain, the smell of red roses in my garden, and the laughter of children playing. To me, the sweetest word in the English language is *grandma*. It is a precious feeling to enjoy the warmth of the love of my life, Gary's hand in mine. We enjoy walking around our neighborhood, greeting many friends and neighbors who respond with kindly waves and words of affection.

I know the future also harbors hardships for me that will inevitably come. I learned this from the past which gave up many in abundance. My memories of them have prepared me for these future encounters by teaching me skills I can use to navigate through the most dangerous storms. Although I have acquired them by living through tragic circumstances, I am grateful for the experiences that contributed to the life I now have and brought me to know the love of our Savior, Jesus Christ.

One such experience came last year. Gary and I learned about a place in a third world country where the river water was polluted. During the rainy season, mud and debris, as well as sewage from cattle and other animals, is carried by floods into the river. This is the only source of water for the people living in the area. The contaminated water causes illnesses such as typhoid and malaria that regularly take the lives of many. After the rainy season ends, the land becomes consumed by drought. Reduced water supplies become even dirtier. Scarcity and contamination worsen.

Through an educational program, we became acquainted with a family living in this area. They shared with us the hardships of the people in this region. Political conflicts, crime, inflation, and food insecurity added to the community's burdens. Our hearts ached as we heard about their trials and the suffering of their children. Over the next two years, we developed close bonds with this family, and they became an important part of our lives. Through helping them, they were able to help many others.

We discovered that like ourselves, they had strong testimonies of our Lord and Savior, Jesus Christ. They believed in His birth, atonement, and resurrection. They were very active in helping and serving others and had adopted children from a neighboring village. Our lives were blessed by our relationship with them. With their help, we were able to secure a small piece of land and make the arrangements to put in a well. A survey was taken, and a time to drill the well was scheduled. They were so excited and shared the date with us.

We replied with this message:

"On that day, Nov. 4, twenty-nine years ago, our beautiful son, Jared died at the age of fourteen. He lives with our Heavenly Father now. Every year on his death date, we try to do something good to remember him. How appropriate that the well waters will come forth out of the ground on that day as a symbol of the living waters of Christ and His glorious resurrection that through Him, all shall live again."

The happy day came. The rig arrived and began drilling. I received a text that contained a short video of the event. A tall machine was noisily drilling the borehole. As it drilled, water began gushing up from a large ground pipe.

The text read:

"We now have water that we can also give to our community as well."

I cried, feeling the love and joy they expressed for the completion of the well on this exceptional day.

The text continued:

"We feel so special to be a part of this history. We know all is well with you and our Heavenly Father and we are glad to be a part of your family. Even though we haven't met face to face, we know we'll surely meet each other one day and hug each of you, including our brother Jared. Our well is a symbol to us of the living waters of Christ. We will call it *Jared's well*. This is a huge blessing to us and the people in this part of the world. We love you both so much!"

Healing a Broken Heart

I AM IN MY LIVING ROOM writing the end of my story, at least my story until now. Yes, I'm still doing well and happy to be alive. I worked hard, and not only did I get to keep my life, but I now have a better life. Whether you are nineteen or sixty-nine, it is important to live each day to its fullest.

I am still busy dying and getting ready for when I do leave this life. You see, busy dying is the best part of living. Small things matter more. Becoming more organized provided me with increased time to accomplish more tasks. Having added time prevented me from procrastinating things. I achieved items on my bucket list. I became a better friend, wife, and mother. I'm more involved with other people in my church and community. I'm happier, healthier, and have a better attitude about life. The people around me are happier, too. I even wrote a book!

This is my treasure box. It is a reminder of my life's journey and where I will be after this life. The things inside help me to visualize my beliefs, goals, and values of an eternal nature. They are symbols to me of all the good in life.

Here, I will open it and show you what's inside. The first item is a little wooden parrot. It's so cute painted orange with tiny blue, green, and yellow wings. It hung in the center of the necklace Jared gave to me one year for Mother's Day when he was seven years old.

Another treasure, the ring from Aaron. The diamond and gold are still so shiny. It only fits my pinky now.

And this next treasure was picked up from the earth, age unknown. It is my river rock from Juan.

I keep things that remind me of the people I love, and who loved me, too.

Yes, you guessed right. I have a lot of boxes full of other treasures from people.

I now have a healed heart that was once badly broken. My physical heart is now functioning well. It was also emotionally broken. When I became busy dying, the same process helped me to release the past. Making peace with death gave me new beginnings.

Gary's calling me. "Kathy, I'm out here on the porch swing if you want to join me."

"I'll be right there, honey."

I carefully place the box back on its shelf in the china hutch. I pause for a moment as I glance at a few things in the room. By the piano that was my mother's is my trumpet from John. Above the fireplace hangs a picture of Gary and me that we had taken while we served an educational church mission. Hanging on the wall is a violin that Jean had practiced repairing when she was studying to be a luthier. Maisie decorated it with beautiful decals, silk flowers, and adorned the bow with a large red silk rose and ribbons. We displayed it at Jean's funeral last January.

I open the front door and sit by Gary on our comfy porch swing.

The sun is casting its bright rays upon a large leafy apple tree that is currently housing a nest of newly hatched hungry robins. Their mother has just returned with a juicy worm dangling from her beak. Our green grass is edged in yellow and purple irises. Our neighbor, Ben, is walking his energetic golden retriever. Oscar is a friendly dog who likes to meet and greet everyone. Our neighbor's two young boys are eating red popsicles as they hurry to meet more children from our neighborhood. Several tiny hummingbirds are lingering in our clematis blooms. The world outside is full of the promise of spring and the bounty of new life.

I enjoy being here with Gary while he holds my hand in his. The warmth of life is everywhere around us.

He leaned over and gently kissed my forehead. "We made it through this. We always do."

The End

Acknowledgements

Richard Paul Evans for his incredible workshops, Ranch Writer Retreats, and encouragement through monthly calls. He is not only a wonderful mentor, but treasured friend—Richard makes everyone feel like he is their friend.

Diane Glad, Richard's assistant and one of the sweetest people I have ever met. I appreciate her friendship and encouragement throughout the entire process of our Ranch Retreats. She makes everything better and she has a special place in my heart.

Debbie Rasmussen for her content editing, and her mentorship while I have walked through this entire publishing process. Debbie was my first contact in Author Ready on our Tuesday night calls and I have appreciated her encouragement as well as the support and comradery of the entire Tuesday night writers' group. She is an amazing person and my dear friend.

Gary Rose, my dear husband, my rock, my best friend, and greatest champion.

Maranda Hawkes, my beautiful and creative daughter.

Rich Hawkes, my loving son-in-law.

Penelope and Matilda Hawkes, my two amazing granddaughters.

Sami Rose, my fun loving and talented son.

Jared Budzenski, my precious son who lives in Heaven.

Tom McFarland, Darla McFarland, and Michelle Tew, my dear siblings.

Colleen Flint, my wonderful, lifelong friend.

Mary Angel Flint, the angel who encouraged me to write.